Neuro-Learning:
Principles from the Science of Learning on Information Synthesis, Comprehension, Retention, and Breaking Down Complex Subjects

By Peter Hollins,
Author and Researcher at
petehollins.com

Table of Contents

Neuro-Learning: *Principles from the Science of Learning on Information Synthesis, Comprehension, Retention, and Breaking Down Complex Subjects* 3

Table of Contents 5

Chapter 1. The Learning Brain 7
   Brain 101 17
   Memory 101 27
   The Learning Success Pyramid 36

Chapter 2. Information Absorption. 45
   Lighten the Load 48
   Chunk It Down 65
   The Healthy Brain 73
   Mix Styles and Mediums 78

Chapter 3. Information Synthesis . 107
   Bloom On 109
   The SQ3R Method 119
   Self-Explanation 137

Chapter 4. Information Retention 155
   Make It Emotional 156
   Active, Not Passive 172
   Spaced Repetition............................ 176

**Self-Testing and Retrieval Practice
.... 186**

Summary Guide.................................... 197

Chapter 1. The Learning Brain

If you've spent even a little time in school during the last few decades, the following scenario will likely be very familiar to you: you need to prepare for a test, so you commit to sitting down for a few hours with your books. You go over the material again and again, trying to drill the facts into your head so that you can recall them later. Maybe you read written sections over and over or try rewriting or reciting the material out loud, as though you were a sponge trying to absorb as much as possible. At the end of the preparation phase, there is more highlighted in your notes than not, and your memory retention is questionable. You do feel pretty good about yourself though, and you even pulled an all-nighter trying to cram the information into your noggin. People will be suitably impressed with you.

The rest of the scenario is also probably familiar—i.e., the part where you walk into the exam room and can only recall a small part of what you "learned" anyway.

And yet, you probably also know someone who excelled at school and just seemed to have a knack for remembering *everything*, absorbing it all with ease and having it stay in there well after the exam came and went. They may have even done this with fewer hours spent studying. While you were inside highlighting the same passages with red, yellow, and green, they were outside riding their bike or engaging in a hot dog eating competition. Why? How? That's not fair.

This book tries to answer those questions and look not just more closely at the methods for learning and memorization we've all been taught, but a little deeper at the neuroscience behind how your brain takes in, organizes, and holds onto new information that you give it. The truth is that we can optimize abstract functions like memory, recall, and information processing by looking at the very concrete, physiological basis they have in the brain itself. Armed with this knowledge, we can work with our brains to their greatest potential, in much the same way as an understanding of anatomy and biology helps an athlete perform at their physical peak. You may have underperformed academically or can't seem to keep it together for your job, but that's entirely changeable.

You've probably felt the limits of your own cognitive capacity at times before and desperately tried to push past them. But rather than doubling down on the same old tactics we've been taught at school, this book tries to understand the brain's natural capacities in order to work *with* them. A brain that is better able to take in information, process and analyze it, and recall it is always going to be an effective, powerful brain. And it's hard to overstate the value of such an asset, whether that's at school, at university, in your career, or in life in general.

In 1953, Henry Molaison lost his mind—well, part of it anyway. (You might recognize Henry from his more anonymous yet infamous moniker of Patient H.M.) In a desperate attempt to stop steadily worsening seizures, Henry's doctors decided to carefully remove two thumb-sized pieces from either side of his brain, in an experimental procedure. Though the seizures did indeed stop, Henry was left with a permanent type of amnesia. New memories were impossible for him to form. He could meet a new person, and if they left the room and reentered, he would behave as if it were the first time he'd ever seen them. Henry Molaison's long-term memory wasn't affected. And he kept his personality and skills intact, even learning rudimentary new skills in the moment (most motor-skill based)—he just never had the memory of having learned them.

What was a tragic outcome for Henry Molaison was an interesting new beginning in neuroscience. Here was proof that the function of memory was explicitly tied to discrete, physiological areas of the brain. A handful of other patients underwent the same procedure, and in each case the doctors discovered that memory was always affected when portions of the medial temporal lobe were removed. The more of this tissue that was removed, the more extensive the impairment to the patient's memory. This was a turning point in understanding the function of the brain, and it's integral to our understanding of neuro-learning.

It's many decades later and neuroscientists now know that an important part of the medial temporal lobe, the hippocampus, is responsible for turning our passing perceptions in the present moment into fixed memories that we can later recall. The hippocampus is the structure that creates memories, and without it, we can have a full, rich experience of the present moment—but be able to return to it again in the form of "stored" memories.

Let's return to the question of cramming before an important exam. Knowing that the brain is directly responsible for the extent to which we can remember things, in a physical way even, how can we make sure we're doing what we can to learn better? How can we understand the process of neuro-learning and how to better cater to what our brains prefer and will accept? What principles can we use to improve our performance on that exam but also transfer to learning in general?

It's important to break down the process of learning into a few distinct aspects. Your brain is performing countless complex procedures every time you speak, read, recall a memory, or comprehend a new concept, but in essence, all of learning can be broken down into three functions.

The first is information *absorption*. This is probably obvious. You cannot begin to talk about how your brain retains and processes information if you don't understand how it's taking that information in first. Simply, we can't learn without the first crucial step of absorption. We need to accurately perceive what's in front of us and be able to pay attention long enough to the relevant details to have it all sink in. For example, if you were trying to learn and master the game of chess, the very first thing you'd need to do is actually hear or read the rules of the game. You'd need to be able to focus and pay attention so that this information could properly be absorbed. You need the energy, lack of stress, and engagement. Information just has to make it inside your head somehow first, and then we can manipulate and solidify it.

Many people falsely believe they have terrible memories when in fact they would have great memories if only they spent enough time *paying attention to* the thing they wanted to remember in the first place. If you've ever "forgotten" some crucial piece of information, or something someone said, you may have actually failed to absorb that data simply because you were attending to something else in that moment. You might forget your keys on the counter not because your mechanisms of memory aren't working, but because you were paying attention to your phone at the moment you would ordinarily reach for your keys, and thus you "forgot" to pick them up. We'll see later on in the book how this step of learning is even more important, and it's not merely whether you're paying attention or not, but the state of mind you're in when you pay attention.

The second aspect of how the brain learns is information *synthesis*, which is how your brain analyzes, processes, manipulates, and understands the information you took in during the absorption phase. In fact, your brain is constantly interpreting the world around you. It has to—there is simply a constant, overwhelming flood of information for every sense out there in the world. Our brain's job is to constantly sift and filter through this, decide what everything means, and put sensations into context.

Even as you read these words, consider the whole universe of sensory data out there that you are carefully ignoring so that you can focus on just the few sensations you're interested in. Consider also how fast your brain must be working to decipher these random black marks into meaning, sifting and sorting, pulling on memory banks so that you understand and can create a picture in your mind of the words "memory" and "bank," for example. Synthesis is making meaning and attaching significance to information in a way that your brain can understand it.

To return to the chess example, you can listen attentively as the rules are explained to you, but at some point, your brain is going to start putting all the pieces together. You might start to wonder if you can move knights a particular way and rooks a particular way or what happens if both pieces encounter one another in such-and-such a layout on the board. Now you're beginning to actually understand the information you've taken in. You're turning those rules over in your head, seeing when and how they apply, testing the limits of the game, and trying to actually comprehend the field of your possible "moves."

Of course, chess is one simple example, but we are all doing this all of the time, whether it's playing chess or learning more complicated "games" like how to pass an exam, how to fill out your tax form, or the best way to drive into town given the traffic jam you know is there. Absorption without synthesis is akin to information that goes in one ear and out the other, while synthesis without absorption is, well, not possible.

The final aspect of the learning brain, and perhaps the most important, is information *retention* (i.e., memory). In effect, we can't really be said to have learned anything if we can't remember anything about the mastery we've gained. As you look at the chess board, you need to draw on your memory of all the different moves each piece can make, as well as the memory of the games you've played in the past and all the lessons and tricks you gleaned from them. Without that knowledge, you can't play effectively. In fact, no skill or knowledge at all is useful if it cannot be recalled at will outside of the moment you experienced it first. Retention without synthesis means incorrect information is probably being acted upon.

Thus, learning comes down to these three key aspects, and we'll devote a significant amount of time to each shortly. Every step depends on the proper functioning of the others: absorption, analysis, and retention. They must work in sequence, or the next step will be built upon a house of cards. And remember, it's the hippocampus's roles in the memory aspects of learning that we are interested in with this book. We'll also be looking at neuroplasticity—i.e., the ability the brain has to change and make new neural pathways when it learns and forms new memories. By understanding the way the brain does this naturally, we can work to enhance the process and generally tap into the learning brain that you already possess.

Brain 101

To understand the nature of neuro-learning, it is helpful to have the basic orientation on how the brain is constructed. We'll try to keep this part short and snappy—it's important for background, but you don't necessarily need to know the *whys* if you follow the guidelines later in this book. It's mostly a battle of two brains, as you'll read.

The *cerebral cortex* is probably the most recognizable part of the brain, as we've seen the brain depicted in biology textbooks—the gray matter that physically resembles a thick sponge. The cerebral cortex is the processor of thought, reason, language, and general consciousness. It may help to assign a so-called avatar to each portion of the brain, and since this portion is focused on analytical thought, this is the *Albert Einstein* portion. It is further divided into four subcomponents called *lobes*.

- *Frontal.* The front part of the cerebral cortex processes reasoning, expression, and body movement. This is where information synthesis occurs.

- *Parietal.* The middle of the cerebral cortex processes sensory information like touch, pressure, and pain. This is where information absorption occurs.

- *Occipital.* The back of the brain covers visual information we receive through the eyes. This is also where absorption occurs.

- *Temporal.* The bottom part of the cerebral cortex handles the interpretation of sounds and language through the *primary auditory cortex* and also processes memories through the *hippocampus*. This is where information retention occurs.

It may seem that the brain has all the components to make learning effortless and easy, but wait, there's more. There's a significant portion of the brain that actively works against our best interests much of the time, and it is known as the *limbic system*.

This is a complex series of parts that conduct all matters involving emotions, stimulation, and memories. It's often the part of our brain that we want to shut off because it is behind most of our fears and anxieties. As such, we can think of an avatar for the limbic system as an easily spooked and skittish cat who runs from everything and everyone. At this point, it's pretty tough to absorb, synthesize, retain, or even think straight. Major components of the limbic system include the following:

- *Thalamus.* A mass of gray matter resting between the two halves of the brain, the thalamus relays sensory and motor signals, which help regulate the body's circadian rhythms and functions like sleep. This can create distraction from your learning activities.

- *Hypothalamus.* Positioned directly below the thalamus, the hypothalamus controls responses to hunger and thirst, emotions, body temperature, and the automatic nervous system. How can you focus if you're too cold or hungry?

- *Amygdala.* A tiny oval inside each of the brain's hemispheres, the amygdala is the hothouse for emotions, survival instincts, memories, and sex drive. Learning and emotion don't play well together, as one requires focus and the other demands it.

Also part of the limbic system is the *hippocampus*, which we mentioned earlier. The hippocampus's main objective is the formation and long-term maintenance of memories. As such, a useful avatar would be the elephant, known for its memory abilities. So why is the hippocampus grouped in with the parts of the brain that are counterproductive? Because memories are not only conscious pieces of information; they are also subconsciously coded and contain multitudes of emotion.

Learning effectively really comes down to a battle of two brains: the prefrontal cortex and the limbic system.

The prefrontal cortex is probably where most of us "exist" in our minds: the conscious and analytical part of us that makes choices based on the information we've obtained. It's the hub of "free will" and our personality development, including decision-making, planning, and thought and analysis. It's like the conference room of the mind.

The prefrontal cortex is where we try to organize our behavior and thoughts with the goals we've set up. It's typically associated with "executive function"—where we make judgments and decisions and formulate strategies to align our actions with our "beliefs," like moral or value judgments (good vs. bad, better vs. best), qualitative assessments (similarities and differences), consequential thinking (what will happen if certain actions are taken, what's the predicted outcome), and social behavior. We use the prefrontal cortex to predict stock market rises, strategize marriage proposals, figure out if we're going to dress up like a unicorn, and decide where to get lunch.

If we're pondering the possibilities of neuro-learning, the prefrontal cortex is where we begin and end.

Unfortunately, it's clear that not all of our intentions translate into actions, and our tendency to act against our best interests is due to the *other* brain.

Our prefrontal cortex is in a constant battle with the limbic system—the part of the brain that's unconsciously dictating our actions by focusing on fear, survival, needs, risks, and desires. The limbic system thinks it is still the year 10,000 BC and hasn't updated itself despite the world around it changing dramatically.

The limbic system is always watching out for us, which is great in theory, but it can also be unnecessarily restrictive. Imagine how phobias and anxiety can derail you despite your best intentions—those are both the result of the limbic system not being adequately balanced by the prefrontal cortex. Both the prefrontal cortex and the limbic system very badly want to make our decisions for us, and as such, they're frequently battling each other for that responsibility. It's your good old-fashioned conflict between logic and emotion.

This struggle is what makes learning so difficult. As your prefrontal cortex is making evidence- and logic-based decisions, your limbic system hijacks that process with its emotional response. When the limbic system overrides the reasoning abilities of the prefrontal cortex, it results in the formation of bad habits or simply distracts you from information absorption.

One function of the limbic system that can create chaos despite its best intentions is the *fight-or-flight* response. This subroutine happens whenever the brain encounters a frightening situation and is forced to decide whether to stay and confront the problem or get the heck out of Dodge and seek safety. The fight-or-flight response emerges from several different kinds of threats: an oncoming car (flight), a stovetop kitchen fire (fight, hopefully), a snarling attack dog (could go either way), or a vindictive father-in-law knocking at your door with a shotgun (you're on your own).

In a suddenly stressful situation, the body releases hormones that signal the body's sympathetic nervous system, which alerts the adrenal system to release hormones that spur the chemical production of adrenaline or noradrenaline. This causes the body to feel certain physical symptoms (high blood pressure, increased heart and breathing rates). The body doesn't return to "normal" until between 20 and 60 minutes after the threat goes away.

Obviously, the fight-or-flight response is key to one's ongoing survival—but it also has certain drawbacks. Most troublesome is the fact that it doesn't differentiate between *actual* threats or just *perceived* ones. Yes, it reacts to a speeding car going through an intersection and heading straight toward you. But it also reacts to misinformation that perpetuates fear of unrealistic events: the recurrence of diseases that have been cured, a swarm of killer bees, a zombie apocalypse, or a piano falling from a tall building. These just don't happen, not even the zombie apocalypse. And the limbic system's inaccuracy about such potential events is what leads to the development of phobias, which have an oversized influence on the super-reasonable prefrontal cortex.

Additionally, the amygdala, that tiny part of the limbic system, also causes some headaches for the prefrontal cortex. Similar to the fight-or-flight mechanism that calls up our survival instinct, the amygdala processes our emotional responses to outside stimulation. Working from information sent from the thalamus through the neocortex, the amygdala decides what emotion to feel and floods the brain with hormones.

This is all fine and well unless the amygdala processes the stimuli as a *threat*, in which case the thalamus bypasses the filtering neocortex altogether and sends info straight to the amygdala. *That* causes the amygdala to become a fight-or-flight arbiter on the spot, which usually leads to emotion-driven decisions—which can be very bad (though not always). The amygdala encourages a response that's more reactive than thought-out. This is when we lash out at a friend or loved one for being five minutes tardy or physically lunge at someone who insults our mother.

One of your brains wants to help you, and the other one wants nothing to do with critical thinking and the learning instinct. But we still haven't quite touched on memory itself yet.

Memory 101

Memory, of course, is heavily related to learning. If memory is a storage system that exists within specific neural pathways, then learning is about changing neural pathways to adapt one's behavior and thinking to the emergence of new information. They depend on each other because the goal of learning is to assimilate new knowledge into memory, and memory is useless without the ability to learn more.

Memorization is how we store and retrieve information for use (essentially the process of learning), and there are three steps to creating a memory. An error in any of these steps will result in knowledge that is not effectively converted to memory—a weak memory or the feeling of "I can't remember his name, but he was wearing purple…"

1. Encoding
2. Storage
3. Retrieval

Encoding is the step of processing information through your senses. We do this constantly, and you are doing it right now. We encode information both consciously and subconsciously through all of our senses. If you are reading a book, you are using your eyes to encode information, but how much attention and focus are you actually using? The more attention and focus you devote to an activity, the more conscious your encoding becomes—otherwise, it can be said that you subconsciously encode information, like listening to music at a café or seeing traffic pass you by at a red light.

How much focus and attention you devote also determines how strong the memory is and, consequently, whether that memory only makes it to your short-term memory or if it passes through the gate to your long-term memory. If you are reading a book while watching television, your encoding is probably not too deep or strong.

Storage is the next step after you've experienced information with your senses and encoded it. What happens to the information once it passes through your eyes or ears? There are three choices for where this information can go, and they determine whether it's a memory that you will consciously know exists. There are essentially three memory systems: sensory memory, short-term memory, and long-term memory.

The last step of the memory process is **retrieval**, which is when we actually use our memories and can be said to have learned something. You might be able to recall it from nothing, or you might need a cue to bring the memory up. Other memories might only be memorized in a sequence or as part of a whole, like reciting the ABCs and then realizing you need to sing it to remember how it goes. Usually, however much attention you devoted to the storage and encoding phases of memory determines just how easy it is to retrieve those memories. Most of the learning process isn't necessarily focused on retrieval—it's focused on the storage aspect and what you can do to force information from sensory and short-term areas into long-term areas.

Think about when you cram for a test. You want information you experience to be in your brain for perhaps 24 hours, which means it has to exist beyond short-term memory and certainly beyond sensory memory. You might not care if you remember this information about the French Revolution at the end of the year, so you will reach a level of attention and focus that will push the information into the hazy area between short-term and long-term memory. In reality, what's happening is that you will rehearse the information enough to make a very faint imprint on your long-term memory.

Improving your learning, in a sense, is the same as improving your memory capacity and how absorbent your memory is—the more sponge-like, the better. However, learning is both the process of improving memory while also getting better at *not forgetting*. Why do we forget? Why can't we remember this fact? How did we ever let something slip from our brains?

As you have read, forgetting is usually a failure or shortcoming in the storage process—the information you want only makes it to short-term memory, not long-term. The problem isn't that you can't find the information in your brain; it's that the information wasn't embedded strongly enough in your brain to begin with.

Sometimes it's easier to think about forgetting as a failure in learning. There are generally three different ways you retrieve or access your memories:

1. Recall
2. Recognition
3. Relearning

Recall is when you remember a memory without external cues. It's when you can recite something on command in a vacuum—for example, looking at a blank piece of paper and then writing down the capitals of all of the countries of the world. When you can recall something, you have the strongest memory of it. You have either rehearsed it enough or attached enough significance to it so that it is an incredibly strong memory within your long-term memory. Of course, because recall represents the strongest level of memory, it's also typically the toughest to achieve. It would typically require hours of rehearsal or study to get anywhere close to this. When we study, we want information to enter this realm, but we will usually settle for the next type of memory retrieval.

Recognition is when you can conjure up your memory in the presence of an external cue. It's when you might not be able to remember something by pure recall, but if you get a small clue or reminder, you will be able to remember it. For example, you might not be able to remember all of the capitals of the world, but if you got a clue such as the first letter of the capital or something that rhymes with the capital, it would be fairly easy to state it. When we cram information, this is typically what we end up with. This is also how mnemonics and similar memory devices work. We know we aren't able to definitively store and recall so many pieces of information with a massive amount of rehearsal, so we work on chunking information into easily recognizable cues.

Relearning is undoubtedly the weakest form of recall. It occurs when you are relearning or reviewing information and it takes you less effort each subsequent time. For example, if you read a list of country capitals on Monday and it takes you 30 minutes, it should take you 15 minutes the next day, and so on. Unfortunately, this is where we mostly lie on a daily basis. We might be familiar with a concept, but we haven't committed enough of it to memory to avoid essentially relearning it when we look at it again. This is what happens when we are new to a topic or we've forgotten most of it already. When you're in the relearning stage, you essentially haven't taken anything past the barrier of short-term memory into long-term memory.

Not only are we fighting weak encoding or storage in our quest for learning, but we are also fighting the brain's natural tendency to forget as soon as possible.

This is encapsulated by the *forgetting curve*, a concept pioneered by psychologist Hermann Ebbinghaus. Below is a picture of the forgetting curve, courtesy of Wranx.com.

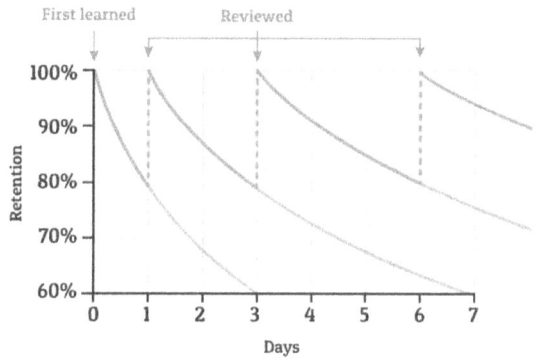

Typical Forgetting Curve for Newly Learned Information

This shows the rate of memory decay and forgetting over time if there is no attempt to move this information into long-term memory. If you read something about the French Revolution on Monday, then it's typically expected that you will remember only half of it after four days and retain as little as 30% at around a week's time. If you don't review what you've learned, it's very likely you will only retain 10% of what you learned about the French Revolution. At some point you might just remember that a short guy named Napoleon was involved.

However, if you review and rehearse it, you can see in the graph above how you will retain and memorize more over time. You will bump the retention level back up to 100%, and then the graph will start to become shallower, indicating less decay.

The goal with the knowledge of the forgetting curve is to make the curve shallower—to make it resemble a horizontal line as much as possible. That would indicate very little decay, and doing that requires constant review and rehearsal.

Ebbinghaus found patterns for memory loss and isolated two simple factors that affected the forgetting curve. First, the rate of decay was significantly blunted if the memory was strong and powerful and had personal significance to the person. Second, the amount of time and how old the memory was determined how quickly and severely it decayed. This suggests there is little we can do about forgetting other than to come up with tactics to assign personal significance to information and rehearse more often.

As you can see, forgetting isn't as simple as having something on the tip of your tongue or rummaging through the stores of your brain. There are very specific processes that make it a near-miracle that we actually retain as much as we do.

Now that you've been inundated with more brain science than you've likely read since high school, let's shift gears and talk about the psychological factors that are key to effective learning. This is nicely summed up in what's called the learning success pyramid. This takes us from the biological processes to the psychological mindsets that help us in our goals.

The Learning Success Pyramid

Legendary college basketball coach John Wooden was also an astute personal philosopher who developed "the pyramid of success." He intended it as a diagram to guide students through 15 different "blocks" on the course to success in their personal and practical ventures.

Wooden's model has been appropriated by several others who have sought to provide roadmaps for success or accomplishment, including educator Susan Kruger. She developed the *learning success pyramid*, which identifies the necessary elements one must bring to ensure accomplishment in learning throughout their life. Thoughtfully, Kruger kept her number of blocks to three, down from Wooden's 15:

- confidence
- self-management
- learning

Confidence. At the base of Kruger's pyramid is the self-conviction that we *can* learn. There's no way around this prerequisite, and brain chemistry has something to do with it.

If one is feeling hurt or mistrusted, or if they're dealing with depression, stress, difficult personal issues, or fear, they don't have any resources left to help them learn. We simply have no mental resources left to actually learn, because we are left dealing with the hamster wheel of anxiety and stress. Taken to the extreme, this can shift your brain into fight-or-flight mode. Just imagine being incredibly frightened by public speaking to the point that you can't function. That's why confidence in learning is important.

If you're running low in this area, be kind to yourself and take steps to affirm your learning abilities. You've learned everything in your life thus far from scratch. You may feel ignorant or that you're not good enough—and that might be true, but it's only a temporary condition.

There's not a single subject you can't understand with perseverance and the occasional stretch of hard work. Resolve yourself to not giving up. Make plans for *how* you will learn. Be forgiving of yourself if you need to take a lot of time and mark your progress as you go along.

If there is a pot of gold at the end of the rainbow, and you don't think you can follow the rainbow, it starts to feel pointless. But if you believe that you can, this belief can carry you through demotivating times. The confidence aspect of learning is what makes it possible that you will even keep reading this book.

Self-management. The next tier in the learning success pyramid is organizing one's time, resources, tools, and communication to ensure effective learning. And once again, this process is dictated by how our brain handles incoming information.

After our emotional centers are done processing new info, the next brain part to receive the data is the front brain, or the prefrontal cortex. This is a bit like our own personal assistant: it handles motor function, memory, language, problem-solving, impulse regulation, social behavior, and a bunch of other cognitive skills. When the front brain is exhausted or depleted, we experience a weariness that prevents us from getting anything done.

This is known as *ego depletion* (this has been recently disproven to some degree, but it is fairly undeniable that the more you have on your plate, the more tired you will grow and the less attention and effort you will put into matters in front of you).

The best way to combat this "brain drain" is by working on self-management skills, particularly organization. This simply means taking a lot of time ahead of any task to set up systems, routines, and actions that will make the task easier to execute on an ongoing basis. Preparation is often the critical difference between success and failure, so it's vital not to rush through it. This is a skill that may have lain dormant since traditional education was all about imposing a rigorous schedule. But since we must become student and teacher simultaneously, we cannot afford to neglect this.

This means putting a framework in place at the beginning that details how you're going to execute. If you're teaching yourself a foreign language, you'd want to make a list of books and online audio resources you'll be using. You might want to make a list of how you'll practice and test yourself—maybe with an online sound recorder or a smartphone. And at the end of the course, maybe you'll translate a hefty amount of English text into the language you're learning.

This step might seem a little laborious, especially when you just want to jump into the material. But it will save a huge amount of time down the road and help you learn infinitely more. Regulating yourself into learning better is important because once you have led the horse to water (once you have found the resources), the horse must drink the water itself (you must do it yourself).

Learning. Well, here you are. This is the third and final step to the learning process: the actual learning. With your confidence and self-management levels up to par, you're all set up to learn.

The thing is, learning itself is not a difficult task. But most people make the mistake of believing that this third stage is where they should begin, rather than addressing their confidence and self-regulation issues. They try to tackle learning Russian or French but don't believe they can do it and don't put together a coherent plan for learning and progression. What hope is there, then? Once you can overcome those hurdles in the learning pyramid, or at least address them, learning becomes possible.

Takeaways:

- To learn better, we need to tap into the learning brain that already exists inside of us. This involves understanding how our brain prefers to accept information and working with it instead of trying to cram information inside it like a clown car. In truth, there are always two brains waging war inside us: the prefrontal cortex, which allows us to learn, and the limbic system, which robs us of our senses. Of course, this is a problem that affects far more about our behavior than learning, but it is the first stop on our journey to neuro-learning.

- In the end, we have three primary areas of focus that we can derive from brain physiology: information absorption (literally being able to process and intake information), information synthesis (the ability to analyze, comprehend, and make meaningful), and information retention (memorization and encoding).
- For the last element of retention, we also dive into the three steps of creating a memory, which are encoding, storage, and retrieval. A failure to satisfy any of those steps will lead to quicker forgetting and the overall feeling that you haven't quite learned something.
- Before we dive into techniques that our brain enjoys, we take a quick look at the psychological prerequisites to learning. This is summed up in the learning success pyramid, where we find that confidence (I can do this) and self-management (I will make a plan for how to do this) are paramount to effective learning. We could even go as far as to say that they are prerequisites to learning; how are you going to learn to

speak Norwegian if you can't create a coherent plan for learning and also believe that it is within your abilities to do so?

Chapter 2. Information Absorption

Let's take a closer look at each of these three elements of learning, starting with information absorption. Though it may seem very simple, this stage is so vital, but it's frequently overlooked.

Many of us take for granted that we're giving good-quality, undivided attention to the thing in front of us, but are we really? When learning something new, we must give ourselves the best chance to succeed by ensuring we're in the right state to "see" it at all. Understanding, remembering... that all comes later. The first and maybe most important step is to make sure our exposure and engagement with new information is everything it should be. This involves your attention span, energy, level of interest (sometimes), and even adequate vision and hearing. Even something as rudimentary as impaired vision can sabotage the learning process right from the beginning.

As the simplest example, if you're trying to study for an exam, don't sit in front of your books with your phone next to you. You may be "reading," but your attention is split, and a portion of it is going to your phone, perhaps another portion to the noises outside, to the TV in the corner of the room, to your growling stomach... This can happen even if you are intently reading, yet all of these elements are still within your eyesight and occupying some small share of your brain's bandwidth. It's like your brain has put them on the back burner for later, when they really shouldn't think about them at all.

By constantly splitting and shifting your attention to your phone's messages and notifications, you turn off the learning process in a small way and ensure that you won't recall all of what you read later on. After all, if you never properly take in this information the first time around, what hope do you have of resurrecting it all a second time or even applying it in real life?

When it comes to learning, distraction is deadly. If you could focus your attentive awareness on new stimuli for a full, uncompromised 10 minutes, it would ultimately be worth more than a whole hour of scattered, divided attention. We need to recognize the limits of our brain and not deliberately set out to sabotage ourselves.

One of the brain's limits is that it cannot store in memory something that isn't properly perceived in conscious attention. We can get around this by deliberately cutting down on distraction and the tendency to split our attention and instead choose to focus fully on the information we wish to absorb. Let's take a look at our brain's limitations and how we can work with them.

Lighten the Load

We know all about distractions, and by and large, the advice regarding them is to use the "out of sight, out of mind" adage. So we won't spend much more time on this angle of learning. You shouldn't be reviewing your notes while simultaneously watching reruns on television. Helpful, right?

For the most part, brain limitations concern the "load" we place on ourselves cognitively, otherwise known as *cognitive load theory*. In other words, cognitive load is the effort used by your working memory system to process incoming information. In the same way that your office desk, workbench, or kitchen countertop only has so much space on it, your working memory is limited in its capacity, and you need to learn to work within those limitations.

When you place too many things on your desk or table, you won't have space to work properly and eventually things will start falling off. The analogy here is that overloading your cognitive workspace will have a similar effect, and you jeopardize your learning or forget things quickly after learning them. If the resources you need to process the information at hand are more than what you realistically have, you'll simply fail to learn or understand that material.

So in trying to optimize our working memory, our goal is to *reduce* overall cognitive load or at least ensure that it is only what we can handle without becoming overloaded. Luckily, there are many ways to work around these natural limitations, and your brain knows a few of these tricks already.

Cognitive load can be divided into three different kinds: *intrinsic, extrinsic, and germane.* They all add up to the total load you place on your working memory, like different kinds of tools you might have scattered on the workbench.

Intrinsic load is a property of the task in front of you and can be understood as its level of difficulty. Doing basic arithmetic has a low intrinsic load while more complicated calculus or engineering problems are going to have a greater load. In other words, a task with high intrinsic load is a big item on your desk and doesn't leave much room for anything else, while a smaller one is easier to manage.

To reduce intrinsic load, you need to find a way of simplifying the material into easier-to-understand chunks or place the material into sequences and segments that are simpler to grasp. In other words, break it down! That huge load is hard to handle as it is, but you can dismantle it and process one piece at a time. Cut paragraphs into smaller chunks or even sentences. Focus on smaller parts of diagrams or graphs first or draw a simplified schematic or outline to explain a more complicated process. Find worked examples to model a good answer or concrete examples that clearly showcase the fundamental principles at hand. This places less cognitive load on you and hence makes it easier for you to absorb and understand challenging work.

As an example, someone might be trying to remember the many complicated steps in the chemical processes in photosynthesis. Looking at the whole thing is definitely overwhelming, but it's more manageable when broken down into smaller chunks. They could study just one part of the process at a time, with pared-down diagrams that show only the barest processes. Next, the chunks could be placed together again and their connections analyzed. It's easier to remember several smaller chunks than one enormous one. In fact, almost every scientific endeavor has proceeded in exactly this manner—with the understanding of small elements helping us grasp the bigger, more complex systems.

Extrinsic load, on the other hand, is not a characteristic of the task itself, but it has to do with *how* it's presented. Data can come to your brain in many different forms, much like a computer can save an image as a .jpeg or a .pdf file. You can represent a concept with an equation, a diagram, a paragraph, a lecture, or an interpretive dance for that matter. Naturally, some formats are going to be a little simpler to understand, and some are going to be *personally* better suited to you than others.

Have you ever had a really bad teacher or a textbook that felt like it was actively making you understand less? This is a classic example of high extrinsic load. Even if the intrinsic load of a task is low, a high intrinsic load can threaten your absorption and understanding of the material. Incompetent teachers can present concepts in a disordered or confusing way. Overly cluttered study notes and textbooks or material with loads of unnecessary and redundant information also have high extrinsic cognitive load.

What can you do in this case? Cut through it all by actively simplifying whenever you can, and you reduce this load. Where you can, change the "format." For example, a student may be trying to learn a new math concept but finds that every read of the (outdated) textbook just makes matters more confusing. She may forego the textbook and turn to short online explainer videos, different "for dummies"-style study guides, or even notes and help from other students who understand the concept. This reduces potential grueling hours spent trying to understand poor materials and cuts to the chase.

Another tip to reducing extrinsic cognitive load is to be "goal-free" in your attitude. Focus only on your current state and how to get to the next state, and don't stress too much about the final stage you're meant to reach (i.e., the goal). This is great for multistage math or programming problems. Stay in a loose, nondirected state for a while and simply become curious about the space of potential options in front of you before trying to jump in and immediately solve the stated problem.

Explore the relevant components. Take a look at the different functions, ask a few questions about how they work, and take things step by step. When you're stuck on a particular outcome, your view narrows considerably and you can close yourself off to avenues of understanding that would otherwise help you understand the problem from a new perspective. Being "goal-free" for a while takes pressure off you and clears your working memory somewhat.

If you're trying to study something and feel like the material is difficult or complex, it is likely high intrinsic load. If you feel, on the other hand, that the explanations are confusing or don't make sense, extrinsic load problems are likely the culprit. Knowing which one you're dealing with will help you decide which approach to take—i.e., chunking and segmenting for high intrinsic load and goal-free working to reduce extrinsic load.

Finally, germane cognitive load, the third type, is the effort you're required to make to consolidate the pieces of information you have into one larger concept (i.e., a schema). We'll explore this third type in the next section on chunking.

This is all a roundabout way of saying that our memories, though amazing in some ways and capable of superhuman feats, are generally pretty fickle. In fact, they're so fragile that sometimes even learning something new can cause us to forget what we previously knew (or thought we knew).

In a study published in the *Journal of Experimental Psychology, Learning, Memory and Cognition*, researchers found evidence that memory retrieval itself is a process that aids in "everyday forgetting." But this is not necessarily anything to be alarmed about. There's a very good reason your brain behaves this way. Old information is likely to interfere with newer, more useful information. As an example, consider the memory of an interesting person you may have met last week. Your brain likely remembered all the relevant information—their name, whether you liked them or not, their overall demeanor. But you probably didn't bother to remember the color of their socks or the precise time of day you encountered them.

A study published in the journal *Nature Neuroscience* showed that when two ideas compete with each other, the brain has trouble with retrieval. To fix this interference, the brain uses several inhibitory mechanisms to help suppress one of the competing ideas, which usually means that old memories fade and new ones are reinforced. Every time you recall the "target memory," you're actually further suppressing the interfering one, essentially shaping the past as you remember it. Again, this is an adaptive process that you *want* to happen. In fact, the handful of people who suffer from the very rare hyperthymestic syndrome literally can't forget—and their lives are complicated to say the least.

But forgetting something in this way doesn't mean it's gone forever. Have you ever been out and about and bumped into someone you recognized but couldn't for the life of you remember who they were or how you knew them? Maybe with time you finally remembered but found it difficult because this person wasn't in their usual "place." Maybe they worked at your gym and you saw them every day behind the reception desk, and though you never had trouble remembering who they were when in that context, your mind drew a blank when you suddenly saw that person walking around in an unfamiliar place.

This shows that retrieval is very context-dependent. You may actually have a lot more mental storage space than you realize, only it's accessed when you're in the same mental place in which you made those memories. We'll look more at how to use this knowledge a little later on.

Your brain is not like a computer, functioning in a linear, cause-and-effect fashion. It wasn't programmed, but evolved, and is a living, fluid entity filled with quirks and idiosyncrasies. And yet, like anything biological, or flesh and blood, there are serious limitations that we must consider and cater to.

Another aspect of the cognitive load is just how long we can *last*. Despite the fact that classes in school can last for an hour or more, humans are not good at paying attention to one thing for an extended period of time. At the biological level, we are programmed to pay attention to multiple things for short periods of time instead of focusing on one object. Of course, we can attribute this to our propensity for staying alive by fleeing at the first sign of danger. This biologically leads to short attention spans, and we must learn to account for this in our learning endeavors.

Multiple studies have investigated exactly how long our attention spans are; in one early study, scientists noticed that the quality of the notes students took during a lecture declined in quality as the lecture went on. This led them to posit that human attention spans were 10–15 minutes long and that we have difficulty paying attention to information after that much time passes.

A different study utilized trained observers to watch students for lapses in attention during a lecture. They noticed peak inattention in three spots: during the initial settling-in period, 10–18 minutes into the lecture, and toward the end of the lecture. Indeed, by the final 10 minutes, they noticed students failing to pay attention as often as every three to four minutes. Their conclusion was that declines in attentiveness occur over time and that there is a certain acclimatization period at the beginning, during which we are particularly susceptible to losing focus.

A third study provided students with clickers to press when they found themselves being inattentive during class. This time, the researchers had students sit in on three different types of classes. Some students sat in on a lecture course, others needed to pay attention to a demonstration, and others were in a question-and-answer session. Each student, regardless of the type of class they attended, was provided a clicker with three different buttons. One was pressed to record a lapse in attention of a minute or less, one was pressed to indicate lapses of two to four minutes, and the other was meant to indicate lapses of attention of five minutes or more. This data was then mapped onto the lecture or demonstration people attended to observe how a lesson's style impacted student attentiveness.

They discovered that lapses in attention were sooner than the 10-minute estimate previous studies would lead people to expect. Inattention spiked in the students 30 seconds after arriving to class, during the "settling-in" period, at 4.5–5.5 minutes into class, at seven to nine minutes into class, and at nine to ten minutes in. Attention of the class as a whole continued to wax and wane with this pattern as the class continued, though there were more lapses in attention toward the end of class, when spikes of inattention could be observed every two minutes.

Perhaps the most interesting finding of this study is that the scientists noted much fewer lapses in attention in the demonstration and question-based teaching styles (an important note for the next chapter). When students were more active participants in their classroom experience rather than passive listeners, they stayed engaged more often and for longer periods of time. Taking one of these classes before a lecture course even made that lecture course easier, and students in that position were found to pay attention for longer periods and lapse less frequently. It seems that active learning engages human attention and refreshes it for subsequent, more passive learning sessions.

In short, humans do indeed have almost laughably short attention spans. No matter how flawed the data or study might be, there is a clear consensus of it being only a matter of minutes. So sitting down for hours, or even all night, while trying to cram information into your brain just isn't going to work. We need to work around this attentional limitation by taking more frequent breaks and simply having the expectation that you can't work like a machine.

Perhaps the easiest way to conceive of cognitive load theory and intrinsic and extrinsic loads is to use the brain as a muscle analogy. Any muscle has limitations, so how do you pace yourself so you learn efficiently and prevent burnout? There are three elements you can manipulate to make sure your load is manageable: *intensity, frequency, and duration*.

Intense, difficult learning depletes your units of energy more quickly than easier, simpler learning material. Similarly, your energy is depleted each time you study, and studying more frequently will deplete your reserves more frequently. It's also true that each minute you study takes a little more energy to keep you going, no matter how easy the material you're learning might be. Consequently, studying for a long period of time inevitably depletes many of your units of energy.

Intensity, frequency, and duration all have to be managed. You can allot 33 units of energy to each, but this is going to wear you down fast.

Intensity can be determined by the difficulty of your topic, but more often than not, it's just about how much effort you have to expend in a given hour. Reading is not so intense, while a practice test is very intense. You can also use this to measure your expectations—if you want to just get by, it will not be so intense, but if you want perfection, expect to expend more effort.

Lowering your expectations lowers your stress level and makes the study session less draining.

Frequency of study is the second factor you need to consider when setting expectations for your progress. Each time you study will drain your energy a little bit, and the more difficult the topic is, the more quickly it will drain your reserves each time. If you aim to study during every bit of downtime you have, it ends up being too much of a good thing, because your brain might not get the downtime it needs to integrate your new knowledge and, of course, the space it needs. Our brains need rest to function! If you feel worn out and unable to think at any point, you might be studying too frequently and should slow down a bit.

As for duration? Well, we already know how lacking our attention spans are, so how much focus should you really put on this? Not much, it turns out.

So for instance, if you focus on only intensity and frequency, intense study sessions every day will allow your mind and body to rest and properly synthesize. If you want to crank up the duration of your sessions, it either needs to be less intense or less frequent—two hours every three days, for instance. Leave your brain the room it needs, and the results you want will follow.

You might be dedicated, but your brain can't match it. It's essential to remember this when managing your own studying and to take it into account when scheduling your own sessions.

Over time, you will be able to find your *Goldilocks zone* where your studying isn't too intense, too frequent, or too long in any single session (keep this concept in mind for later when we cover the Yerkes-Dodson curve). Once you do, you'll be able to balance the three factors to maximize the learning you're capable of doing while preventing exhaustion and burnout.

Remember, the more complex your material is, the more time you will need to devote to studying that subject. The longer you study in a single session, the more time you will need between sessions to ensure complete processing and absorption of what you're studying. You can combine intensity, duration, or frequency, but never all three. Learn smarter, not harder.

Chunk It Down

Another way to reduce the load on our brains is to "chunk" information. Chunking is a simple concept: if you have 10 items and you chunk them together to make two groups of five, your brain can absorb them as fewer items, even though the total information is roughly the same. You spend less energy on recall, your cognitive load goes down—and this means you have more available to push yourself, if you want to. And in fact, this is essentially what the third element of the cognitive load theory is about—**the germane load**.

Chunking can improve your capacity for clear and accurate perception of the data coming through your senses, and it is a smart way to work around the limits of just how much your brain can process. In fact, many people who are naturally adept at developing expertise and learning complex topics may already be unwittingly learning this way, or they at least have taught themselves how. When you were first learning to read, you did the same thing. You realized that all the individual letters came together to form new chunks—words. You learned the letters first, then put them together into chunks. As you became more familiar with the words, you realized that they themselves could be grouped together into chunks—sentences. And sentences could make whole stories.

In each case, the chunked group from the previous level becomes the fundamental unit for the next level. Fluent readers no longer focus on each individual letter or even individual words. When you read these sentences right here, your brain is not massively overworked with the cognitive load of processing each and every letter—even though you found this incredibly difficult at one point. The idea is that experts in any field can use the same process to develop supreme efficiency at any task, including memory.

To the casual observer it may seem like they're performing a miraculous feat by juggling countless details, but really, they have only constructed elaborate hierarchies of chunked information, which means that they're not overtaxing their mental capacities at all. With time, real experts seemingly spend no effort at all on their mastery, even describing it as intuitive or unconscious.

So theoretically, anyone can reach virtuoso level if they understand this process and commit to the hours of practice needed to lay down each of those building blocks over and over. You need to understand the building blocks you're working with and how they're connected. Then you need to practice or drill these chunks until they become automatic.

Chunking certainly reduces cognitive load, but the act of thinking through how you are going to chunk also helps information synthesis and retention—it's most often thought of for retention, in fact. It's pretty neat. Let's look at some concrete ways you can use chunking in your own life and in learning.

The easiest and most obvious way to use chunking is to transform X amount of information into <X units of information, and the way to do that is typically through grouping, categorization, and pattern-seeking. These are the most rudimentary and effective ways to reduce the cognitive load by flipping the perspective through which you view the information in front of you.

Grouping: For instance, birthdates are never written as 03161986; instead based on grouping, they are chunked as 03/16/1986, or March 16, 1986. A random string of letters such as IKNOWTHISISRANDOM can become I KNOW THIS IS RANDOM. You just arbitrarily group or divide the information and make it meaningful to you.

Categorization: You can use the same strategy for things such as shopping lists, such as by categorizing the items by use, dish, or type of food. A list of tomatoes, garlic, olive oil, ground beef, soy sauce, wasabi, raw fish, and ginger has eight elements, but in reality, there are two obvious categories: pasta sauce and sushi.

Pattern-seeking: To use patterns in chunking, you are finding or imposing a rule that applies to everything in the information you want to reduce the load for. This would also even allow you to predict what may arise in the future regarding this information set.

Chunking is a much deeper rabbit hole, however. Recall that chunking essentially works by reducing memory load, and another way to do this is to replace short-term memory items with long-term memory ones. Why is it easier to remember words in your own language than in a foreign language? Well, because when you remember a word like "dog," you're actually conjuring up a long-term memory of what that word means. Try to remember a nonsense word like "jarlkit" and it takes more effort since you have to use your working memory to break it down into its letter components first.

You have an enormous long-term memory but a relatively small working memory—think of it like a vast library or warehouse of data compared to one small work desk. The more you can store away in the library (with a proper filing method so you can retrieve it later!), the more space you have in working memory and the more you'll remember overall. You want to compress skills, information, or sensations into smaller and smaller subcategories, then learn to retrieve the entire category at will.

First, identify and master the fundamental subskills of what you're trying to learn or the units of information you're trying to remember. You can't learn the piano all at once—first master scales and how to read music. You can't learn to play chess all at once—first master smaller moves and dynamics before looking at entire games. Similarly, don't try to learn the entire anatomy of the brain, but first learn about smaller regions and how individual neurons work. This is called pretraining, and it's a vital part of the learning process. Breaking things into smaller units in general will help your learning and also give you the proper kindling for building your chunks.

Very often, difficulty with a subject comes down to incomplete pretraining in any case: struggling with trigonometry may be because basic geometry hasn't been mastered, and a course on genetics will be too difficult if some fundamental biology concepts are missing from your training. The popular mnemonic technique is an excellent example of chunking in action. If you had to remember a list of words or names, you could instead remember the first letter to each, then arrange those letters so that they spell a single word that's easier to remember. Now, rather than the cognitive load of remembering all those words, you simply have one word to remember. Another technique is to group items by meaningful category. It's easier to remember a list of animals if you know that you have three birds, three fish, and three mammals on the list.

Another great technique is to "map" information onto old memories. For example, you might be trying to remember a complex sequence of events for a history exam. You could assign each main event to a room in your house. You will never forget the order of rooms through which you walk around your house, so remembering the events in order is simply a matter of assigning the right event to the right room. Assign some key points to remember to items in each room; for example, you can remember the publication of an important 1830 treatise by chunking that information to long-term memories of your kitchen. You remember "treat"ise by associating it with the "treats" in your pantry and convert the year 1830 into a time—the time in the evening you usually get yourself a little snack.

There really is no limit to *how* you chunk. In fact, the more emotionally charged or personally meaningful a particular association or way of chunking is, the better. Your brain can easily remember stories, associations, complex narratives, and more, but it finds it hard to juggle meaningless chunks that don't connect to each other in any logical way. So help your brain out by making chunks where you can.

The Healthy Brain

Finally, when it comes to optimizing your brain's capacity to absorb information properly, there is one point that can't be ignored: the actual physical health of your brain itself. It might seem obvious, but it's something many of us forget sometimes. If the tool you need to help you absorb new information is compromised somehow, then its efficiency is compromised, and it doesn't matter how sophisticated your learning techniques are. If you have a laptop that you regularly spill coffee over, it won't matter how great the software installed on it is—it will probably not work very well over time, if at all.

Getting enough restorative sleep, keeping good fitness overall, and eating properly are all ways to keep in good health, and your brain is naturally a part of this. But let's look at a particularly important factor: *stress*. We discussed this a bit in the first chapter, but to understand why it's so important to managing and moderating stress, we need to understand the difference between the thinking brain and the reactive brain. Your prefrontal cortex, or thinking brain, is about conscious absorption and processing of information, while the reactive brain is about instinctual, unthinking responses to that information.

The thinking brain is responsible for, well, thinking. It processes and filters the billions of pieces of information that are constantly coming at it. Importantly, the thinking brain is only 17% or so of your total cognition. When the thinking brain is in charge, it controls what information gets filtered through, allowing you to proceed through your world calmly, rationally, and deliberately. You get to control what information makes it through to your prefrontal cortex, but that's a tough task in and of itself.

When your stress levels are high, or you're anxious, irritable, or sad, the incoming information is passed through your reactive brain instead of your thinking brain. Your reaction can then be to ignore the unpleasant sensation, fight against it, or avoid it. Rather than truly processing the information, you respond reactively to it, sometimes with more negative emotion and sometimes with behavior that may not be in your best interest.

Every piece of new information, every new memory, must first pass through your brain's emotional core, the limbic system. Here, the amygdala and hippocampus direct incoming information according to your emotional state. Negative emotions hog huge amounts of the brain's resources, and you're essentially in a survival mode. One thing you *can't* do in survival mode is take in new information!

A happy, calm brain, on the other hand, will result in the amygdala routing information to your higher thinking brain instead, resulting in more clarity and better learning. This is why it's critical to become aware of your emotional state and commit to keeping peaceful and calm. Deep breaths, visualizations, and reflection all help you step outside of the stress for a moment.

People learn better when they're calm and happy—so one of your first steps to enhancing your own learning is to spend a little time on your mindset.

But actually, everyone has an optimal level of stress and arousal that is motivating. It turns out that zero stress is not a good thing either.

This level is achieved when you are alert and engaged but not overly fearful. You're aiming for a slight challenge out of your comfort zone, but not something that appears impossible. Let's suppose you are tasked with writing a paper on turtles. By some twist of events, you happen to be an expert on turtles. You are confident in your ability to answer questions about turtles. Is your current level of arousal going to be motivating? It might not be, because it's too easy. You'll push it to the side because you'll be bored of it. Now what if the subject was ancient Greco-Roman wrestling? Well, you know what happens when we get too stressed or worried.

These two topics illustrate the zones of demotivation, where we are either too stressed and aroused to function or not stressed and aroused enough to care. The balance between these extremes is the sweet spot where you function at your best and are most motivated. You're a little bit nervous but not too nervous. You're alert but not overly stressed out. This sweet spot is where we must frame learning, otherwise we will fall prey to either one of the extremes.

The so-called sweet spot was defined in 1908 by Robert Yerkes and John Dodson and was developed to understand when people performed optimally. They designed a graph in the shape of an upside-down U that demonstrates how our performance on a task will be poor when we are disengaged (uninterested), but as our arousal rises, our performance improves until it reaches the sweet spot—the Yerkes-Dodson curve. Beyond that point, further arousal becomes a handicap. The stress becomes debilitating, and our performance and motivation suffer.

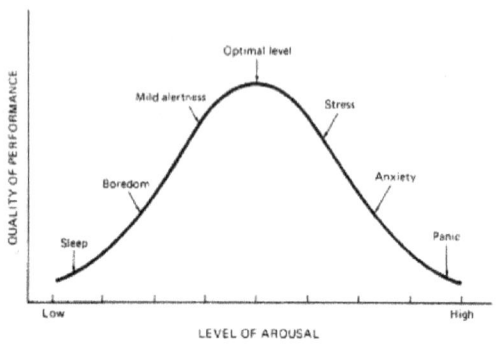

Image courtesy of ResearchGate

A brain on excessive stress is a brain in crisis mode. A brain with a complete lack of stress is a brain that is on vacation. Neither of these are good for your mental performance.

Mix Styles and Mediums

Finally, the last piece of the puzzle for better information absorption is to present the information in different styles, mediums, forms, and all of the above.

When it comes to learning, there are about a million and a half different so-called styles, methods, and mediums, each with their own cadre of advocates using supporting hypotheses. The learning pyramid might be the most infamous one that you have probably heard of (yes, that one was disproven as well). Another one might be the myth about hemispheres having different functionalities, such as the right hemisphere of the brain possessing our creative potential, while the left hemisphere houses the logical aspects. That one has also been disproven.

In reality, this is a relief because it means that information is simply information, no matter how it is presented. There is no need to engage in special formulas or techniques just to optimize learning. Whether you hear information through reading or writing makes no difference to how you process it.

This comes with a rather large caveat.

The notion of different styles and mediums still has quite a bit of merit because learning comes down to how focused you are and how much attention you pay. That's really what determines how much information you can absorb. You can hear a lecture and read a book on the same topic, but if you are constantly distracted while reading the book, you might be better serviced with audio lessons in whatever you want to learn.

Perhaps the important lesson regarding learning styles, approaches, and mediums is that you learn the best in whatever you can pay attention to. When learning becomes tedious and boring, that's when it becomes ineffective. Therefore, we will explore a few different ways for you to absorb information. Ultimately, whatever works best for you is what you should adopt, be it from a disproven myth of learning or a scientifically proven theory. As long as it produces results, either choice is fair.

We'll talk about two models of learning that contain multiple ways of engaging with information. The first is the Solomon-Felder index of learning styles and preferences. It was created in 1996, and it consists of eight approaches to learning information. Again, the purpose is to arm you with different tools you can use, not push one approach over others. Perhaps you can identify which of the following styles you already utilize and consciously step outside of yourself to use the opposing one next time.

The styles, which we will discuss in greater detail, are below. Just because some of the styles appear to oppose others doesn't mean that you can't feel a connection to both or all of them.

- active versus reflective
- sensing versus intuitive
- visual versus verbal/other
- sequential versus global

Active versus reflective. An active learner obtains knowledge by doing. They're constantly interacting with what they're learning by putting it into practice or having exchanges with others where they explain or debate it. Reflective learners are more likely to consider the material they're learning first, analyzing and sorting it out mentally before putting it into action. More concisely put, active learners say, "Let's do something!" while reflective learners say, "Let's think this through!"

Let's take woodworking as an example. An active learner would get all the materials they need, read through some basic instructions, and start putting a table together. They learn a lot by trial and error: finishing the wood surface, cutting pieces, and putting them all together to see how they worked. A reflective learner, on the other hand, might stop after reading the instructions and consider the geometrical strategy, analyze the different kinds of paints and stains they might use, and basically just add more levels of thoughtful planning to *understand* what they want to happen. As long as this part doesn't lead to an unacceptable amount of procrastination, that's fine.

Sensing versus intuitive. This pair of learning styles is related to the dichotomy of "detail-oriented" and "big-picture" thinkers. Sensing learners are attracted to information, memory, and traditional designs of learning—they're practical. They have an eye for specific elements in a task, itemize and follow established problem-solving procedures, and pay close attention to the particulars of a problem.

Intuitive learners, on the other hand, focus on the effects, connections, and potentials of a certain skill. They're creative and seek new prospects for understanding the relationships between concepts. They don't always pay mind to the little details and might make errors more often, but their intense understanding of the goal at hand keeps their perspective vital. They think more abstractly.

For example, a sensing learner in a web development program would focus on all the minutia of their code. They're fastidious about reviewing each line, spotting errors, and making adjustments as needed. They'd know the intimate details of their scripts and would probably know how to fix an error quite quickly. An intuitive learner would be more focused on how certain applications and codes would work together, how the individual cogs relate to each other in service of a bigger purpose. The sensing learner sees HTML code, JavaScript, and individually executable components; the intuitive learner sees the components of an online store and tries to make them all work in sync.

Visual versus auditory versus read-writer versus kinesthetic. These styles are differentiated in the way information is presented to the learner. Visual learners, as you'd expect, respond to pictures, charts, graphics, sketches, movies, live demonstrations, and other eye-friendly media. They learn through seeing things. A visual student of social studies responds to a graph showing population distribution; a visual cooking student appreciates a tutorial video of someone making pan-fried chicken.

We classify two slightly different styles under the heading of verbal learning. Auditory learners learn through hearing and speaking, as in a lecture or discussion group. Their grasp of the Battle of Waterloo is greater when an animated professor is telling the story.

Read-write learners, on the other hand, focus on the written word, retaining information through books, research narratives, and transcripts; written reports or accounts are also their preferred output for explaining what they've learned. They'd prefer to read a book about Napoleon's defeat at Waterloo. Both auditory and read-write learners place heavy emphasis on words.

Kinesthetic learners thrive on physical activity. They need movement. Their muscles are the primary conduits for their memory; they tend to excel at hand-eye coordination, physical timing, and reaction. Obviously, kinesthetic learners tend to excel at sports, dancing, and other physical actions. But astute teachers can instruct more intellectual subjects to kinesthetic learners—for example, by encouraging them to draw diagrams or sketches of what they're learning (it keeps their hands moving).

Sequential versus global. This pair of learning approaches is parallel to sensing/intuitive. The sequential learner needs order and logical procession. They get knowledge in a linear fashion, one piece at a time, and each piece of knowledge is a reasonable extension from the one that came before. Sequential learners solve problems by following a series of ordered directions, advancing within them one by one.

Global learners are less systematic. They learn things on the fly as they occur and can't necessarily describe the smaller particulars of the subject they learn. They tend to respond to leaping from topic to topic, and don't always see how each topic connects at first. But somehow, they eventually "get it." Their natural inclination to learn in a more accidental way allows them to form unusual relationships between individual schools of thought and knowledge, which in turn helps them solve more intricate and complicated issues in unexpected ways.

For example, in learning how to be a better public speaker, a sequential learner would want to progress step by step. They'd take one aspect at a time: writing a speech, changing vocal tone, using gestures, reading an audience—each facet of public speaking would be revealed in logical order and dealt with one at a time. A global learner would fling themselves out there and learn in practice without pondering each step.

They'd dive into public speaking and analyze their overall skills in larger groups, fine-tuning the aspects gradually but separately.

By actively planning your learning, you are putting yourself in the best position for success. Whatever keeps your attention is what causes the best learning.

Next, we turn our sights to the learning pyramid. The learning pyramid is a well-known visual aid that ranks all learning methods in order of how much knowledge students retain using each strategy.

The pyramid suggests that students retain 5% of what they learn in a lecture, 20% from audiovisual sources, 75% in practice, and so forth. The pyramid is divided between passive and active learning, with the top four tiers of lecture, reading, audiovisual learning, and demonstration identified as "passive." The bottom three layers of discussion, practice, and teaching others are described as "active."

It's theoretical, and most education experts dispute its applicability across the board.

There is no real concrete, scientific proof that the learning pyramid is accurate.

Nevertheless, I like the idea. There's nothing in the explanation of the learning pyramid that seems outrageously wrong, and I agree that mixing up mediums of learning is a very good idea. Again, it comes down to what keeps you engaged and focused, and the more active the type of learning, the more engaged you will be. Use all of the types of learning in the pyramid and you are bound to absorb information better—even if only out of novelty and surprise!

Here's a breakdown of each of the tiers of the pyramid.

Listening to lectures (5% retention). The type of learning that has the least effect on memorization is the good ole professor standing at the lectern. This way of learning is increasingly becoming trivial as technology advances. I'm not entirely convinced that's not just an excuse for not showing up to class, but I understand the thinking.

In the specific area of skill acquisition, there aren't a lot of situations where classic lectures are an integral component—perhaps a class instructor explaining the spiritual background of yoga or an auto shop teacher explaining how an engine works. Generally, discourses about the theory of a certain skill are limited to the very beginning of your instruction. Theory is helpful and important to know, but only for background, context, and general comprehension of significance.

Reading (10% retention). There's no question that reading books about a certain subject, especially ones about the skill you're learning, is a vital component. You can find plenty of publications that contain valuable information: how-to books on carpentry, step-by-step manuals on self-defense, strategic volumes on real estate negotiating, even regular periodicals on fishing and landscaping. It's always better to have too much information handy than not enough.

But all the reading in the world by itself may not help you master a skill. You'll have to put it into practice. Even though reading is defined as "passive" learning, one needs to make it as active as one can by connecting the material you're reading to your own ideas, observations, and life experiences. That's true for all reading.

Audio/visual learning (20% retention). This is learning by watching or listening to programs about your topic of interest—perhaps books on tape about political history for those trying to build up debate skills or YouTube demonstration videos on cooking.

You can access enough audiovisual material over your phone and laptop—even your car. It's certainly true that online course modules like Udemy and Coursera offer A/V materials in a very organized fashion for the topic or skill you want to learn. I'm skeptical it's that much more memorable than active reading, but I agree that, as a passive learning plank, it's a good one. Strictly defined, a skill is *doing something*, so it's great to watch someone because it's easier to directly emulate them.

Demonstration (30% retention). This is the live performance of a certain task right in front of you, like a cooking demonstration at a supermarket or welding wires together with a soldering iron. Demonstrations are the heart of private lesson teachers and adult classes. They're obviously more memorable than prerecorded A/V materials because they happen right in your presence and you can actually ask questions of the person doing the demonstration. It's a big building block of mentoring and coaching, where you're shown how to do something and then compelled to do it yourself.

Group discussion (50% retention). This is the first example of active learning in the pyramid, where you converse with a few others who are learning the skill you're taking up. This could be a roundtable with green thumbs who are trying to build a vegetable garden from scratch or a group of Spanish language students who get together and practice with each other. You are able to exchange ideas and thoughts and clear up misconceptions as they occur. You can compare experiences. A writing group, for example, can reveal how other writers approach the same subject from different points of view, raising questions about the subject you may not have thought about.

In particular, discussing your skill with people of different levels—both above and below you—facilitates better practicing and comprehension. When you seek to teach someone less skilled or knowledgeable, you can organize your thoughts and simplify matters for yourself. When you seek to learn from someone more skilled or knowledgeable, well, that's the whole point.

Real-life experience (75% retention). Getting under the hood of the car to perform maintenance, knitting a sweater, playing piano to an audience, building a treehouse—actually using your hands to finish a task is the surest way to master it over time. These examples reinforce how your skill actually gets executed in the real world, not in a theoretical or abstract way.

You get a better understanding of the real purpose of your skill and learn firsthand how to handle stress and solve problems in an unambiguous manner. All the reading and lectures in the world won't quite do simple hands-on experience justice.

Teaching others about your real-life experience (90% retention). The learning pyramid maintains that the best way to retain what you learn is by becoming a teacher yourself, in a sense. This could be giving a talk on your experiences as a mountain climber or starting a blog about filmmaking techniques you've employed. By verbalizing your experience, you help it resound with yourself as well as others.

When you articulate the methods you use and the experience you obtain, you find out what you know and don't know in quick order. As you become aware of these issues and solve them, you're able to organize your own thoughts much more effectively than when you began.

Without a doubt, teaching is one of the most involved, participatory, and non-passive types of interactions with new information we can have. Like self-explanation and the Feynman technique (covered in a later chapter), teaching someone not only roots information in your mind, but also forces you to see what you truly can explain and what you can't. Teaching yourself is good; teaching others is even better.

Teaching exposes the gaps in your knowledge. Having to instruct and explain doesn't let you hide behind generalizations: "Yeah, I know all about how that works. I'll skip it for now." That won't fly if you're explaining a process to someone else—you have to know how every step works and how each step relates to another. You'll also be forced to answer questions about the information you're teaching.

Having to explain what's going on is essentially a test of your knowledge, and you either know it or you don't. If you can't explain to someone how to replicate something you are teaching, then you actually don't know it.

Let's take photography as an example. According to the learning pyramid, reading and lecturing combined take up 15% of your retained knowledge, which makes sense: there's only so much you can learn about photography from a textbook or a lecture. Audiovisual aids and seeing demonstrations—what certain angles look like, how to use computers to filter a print—are yet more helpful in learning to take and process certain pictures. A group discussion about photography would unlock some memorable ideas, and of course, spending the time to practice taking and developing pictures makes solid impressions on your experience.

Now let's examine the bottom (or top, depending on your view) part of the pyramid related to teaching others. You're reinforcing the basic knowledge in others and explaining the principles, types, and general guidelines of photography. Theoretically, you're overseeing all the upper (or lower) segments of the pyramid for students and using your knowledge of the photography process as a guidepost for all of them. And this doesn't even include the pre-instruction time when you're preparing for your own class.

All those teaching activities are active agents that call upon what you already know—and the act of pulling something *out* of your brain rather than putting stuff *into* it turns out to be incredibly important in learning, skill acquisition, memory, and any type of improvement.

That's exactly what's happening with the higher levels of the pyramid. You're extracting from your previously learned knowledge, interpreting it, and reshaping it for others to understand and learn. In turn, that reinforces what you know and deepens your experience a little in the process.

It's common that you even surprise yourself and find additional insights by explaining and reasoning out loud in a way that simplifies and condenses. Teaching forces you to create bite-sized chunks and teach replication—a task you may find far different than explaining theories or concepts.

Using these methods and mediums in combination, both from the learning pyramid and the Solomon-Felder index of learning preferences, and getting them to play well together can make for a compelling learning experience that will enrich your understanding, skill, and talent.

Say you want to learn to make sushi. Start with cookbooks and lectures on the theory and history of sushi. Sprinkle in some YouTube videos that show sushi preparation on camera and check out the documentary *Jiro Dreams of Sushi*, which depicts the daily life of one of the greatest sushi chefs in Japan. Any aspiring sushi chef must also attend an up-close demonstration and class, and no doubt you'll be doing some hands-on efforts in that class as well. You can discuss techniques with other people in your class. And when you've gotten enough experience under your belt, you could attempt to teach your friends how to make sushi or make videos yourself.

Joining together all of these various activities into an organized plan is a near-certain way to ensure effective learning and eventual expertise in a skill.

To end this chapter, it might be helpful to touch upon the myth of learning styles as we mentioned earlier. The theory (myth, really) says some students learn better when the material is presented visually, while others prefer verbally, logically, or some other manner.

But does science exist that supports tailoring learning styles? In other words, are some people's brains just wired differently in this regard so that information ceases to become information if it isn't presented in the right style? Well, the learning styles in discussion are well known, and in an anecdotal way, they even make logical sense:

- Visual (spatial): Prefers learning through images, pictures, colors, and maps.

- Aural (auditory-musical): Leans toward learning through hearing sound and music.

- Verbal (linguistic): Chooses to use words, in both speech and writing—books, lectures, etc.

- Physical (kinesthetic): Prefers using the body, hands, and sense of touch. Typically enjoys sports and exercises.

- Logical (mathematical): Favors logic, reasoning, and systems, particularly finding patterns and connections between unrelated elements.

- Social (interpersonal): Likes to learn in group settings with open communication and exchange with others.

- Solitary (interpersonal): Tends to be more private and independent as well as self-reflective and personal.

It's not a stretch to say that some students consciously *like* some ways of learning over others. I certainly enjoy some activities better than others and, in doing so, may create a self-fulfilling prophecy for myself based on enjoyment. There are even some biological factors that appear to support the theory, as there are different brain structures for each of these types of functions that the learning style corresponds to:

- Visual: The occipital lobes at the back of the brain manage the visual sense.

Both the occipital and parietal lobes manage spatial orientation.

- Aural: The temporal lobes handle aural content. The right temporal lobe is especially important for music.

- Verbal: The temporal and frontal lobes, especially two specialized regions called Broca's and Wernickeï's areas.

- Physical: The cerebellum and the motor cortex (at the back of the frontal lobe) handle much of our physical movement.

- Logical: The parietal lobes, especially the left side, drive our logical thinking.

- Social: The frontal and temporal lobes handle much of our social activities. The limbic system (not shown apart from the hippocampus) also influences both the social and solitary styles. The limbic system has a lot to do with emotions, moods, and aggression.

- Solitary: The frontal and parietal lobes, and the limbic system, are also active with this style.

But?

There's no actual scientific evidence to suggest that the brain works in such fragmented ways. The only data produced to support the theory is presented by poorly run studies or misinterpretation of certain conclusions. The myth—or *neuromyth*—of learning styles is starting to meet more resistance lately, but there's still an adherence to the idea. In fact, there's plenty of evidence to suggest that all learning styles are equally effective when you account for attention and preference.

Paul Howard-Jones, a researcher at Bristol University, said that tailoring learning styles and other neuromyths are "misconception(s) generated by a misunderstanding, a misreading, or a misquoting of facts scientifically established by brain research to make a case for use of brain research in education or other contexts."

There's a risk in assuming that there's only one style that we should adhere to. We'd be doing a disservice to our range of ability and missing out on other potentially effective methods and mediums. Such an opinion tends to become a self-fulfilling prophecy in that you'll only pay attention to one method and reject the others. That can only work to your detriment.

If you seek to learn in only one style, your options will be limited. Your options may even be terrible, whereas materials in other styles might be far superior. There is also the benefit of mixing and matching different types of media to gain full perspective of whatever you are trying to learn.

This same approach can be used in any subject that's got enough audio, visual, and textual content to use in learning. Frankly, there aren't many that don't. History, mathematics, foreign languages, music, and even practical arts like woodworking or computer skills all have various forms of media with valuable information.

Incorporate it into your study plans as much as you like, and don't feel the need to chain yourself to a categorization that has no scientific basis, no matter how logical it may appear to be.

Takeaways:

- Information absorption is the first key to effective learning that caters to our brains. If we cannot see, hear, or perceive a piece of information, forget about the rest of the process. No number of memory techniques or amount of deep learning will make a difference if the information hasn't made it into your head.

- The first step to ensuring that we can properly absorb information is to look at the cognitive load that we place on our brains. There are three types of loads: intrinsic, extrinsic, and germane. They have to do with how difficult the information is, how the information is present, and how difficult the information is to turn into something with personal significance. The brain is mighty, but still biological and in need of plenty of rest, breaks, and light cognitive loads. Another way to look at it is that we can only choose two of the following three elements: *intensity*, *frequency*, and *duration.*

- Chunking is a magnificent way to lighten the cognitive load and assist in information absorption because it literally turns 10 pieces of information into three (for example). The simple ways for chunking to help all three elements of the learning process are to chunk based on groupings, categories, and patterns—all of which you can arbitrarily create. Effective ways to chunk information for better absorption and synthesis (and also retention) are to map new information onto old information and tear it down to the smallest subparts possible, which means that you are breaking something down so you can chunk it together in a way that is significant to you.

- Something that makes the brain unable to pay attention, focus, or care about anything at all is stress. We covered this briefly in the first chapter when we looked at the brain's components and the limbic system in particular. When the brain is under stress, everything shuts down. And yet, we cannot function without a small level of stress; this assertion is governed by the Yerkes-Dodson upside-down U curve, which dictates that we all have a so-called sweet spot in terms of stress for best mental performance. Not too much, but not so little so as to stay engaged.

- Finally, when it comes to information absorption, we must be resourceful in finding ways to capture attention and engagement. This is where mixing and matching different learning styles and mediums comes into play. It's not necessarily that any of these styles and mediums are scientifically better than others, but sometimes we can burn out, grow bored, or simply not care when something is presented in a way that we don't like or prefer. Thus, we present a couple of different models for different styles and mediums: active versus reflective, sensing versus intuitive, visual versus verbal/other, and sequential versus global, as well as the dubious knowledge of the learning pyramid, which contains listening, reading, audio/visual, demonstration, discussion, real-life experience, and teaching others. Remember, the myth of learning styles is just that—a myth.

Chapter 3. Information Synthesis

This brings us to the second aspect of learning—and arguably the most complex. Though many of us can learn to absorb information better by simply opening our eyes and paying attention, this next step may prove to be more of a challenge to optimize.

So far, we've spent some time discussing learning in the abstract, or memory in the simple sense of recalling random strings of information. Of course, the real world is far more complicated than this, and beyond grade school there isn't too much of a need to learn "parrot fashion" or memorize data like a machine.

"Learning" is in fact a broad, very sophisticated set of functions, and the ability to synthesize the information coming in is perhaps the most important. You could be perfectly adept at absorbing and remembering information, but what good is it if the information is unclear, irrelevant, or just plain wrong? How do you use that information to actually improve your life? That's a question that cannot be answered with information that has only been absorbed in a shallow way.

In a very real sense, learning is about comprehension. It's about chewing on information and seeing it from all angles. It goes deeper than the symbols meant to portray certain ideas, processes, or connections. Our learning will always be far richer—and more robust—if we can truly grasp it intellectually, process it, interpret it, and in general interact with it actively rather than merely take it in uncritically. So much of learning actually takes place during the synthesis process—even as you read this, your brain is working hard to convert these ideas into *meaning*, into pictures in the mind, into abstract concepts that you have an emotional reaction to.

Synthesis of information entails asking questions, trying to understand what we know, what we don't know, and how to bridge the gaps. It takes context into account, it's adaptive and responsive, and it's curious about its own learning process—i.e., metacognition. This part of the learning process is all about playing with information and seeing it from different angles.

Bloom On

So we come to a tool that is all about interacting with information. It is called Bloom's taxonomy and it was created by Benjamin Bloom in 1956 (though updated in 2001) as a way to measure the academic performance of college students. It has since been a staple in academic institutions to be a framework for crafting lessons that ensure a thorough comprehension in students.

It essentially states that for the highest level of subject understanding, there are six sequential levels we must be able to complete. Most people will never make it through all the levels in the taxonomy, so don't let yourself fall victim to that fate. The current taxonomy's levels are, from lowest level to highest level of understanding, as follows:

- Remember. Retrieving, recognizing, and recalling relevant knowledge from long-term memory.
- Understand. Constructing meaning from oral, written, and graphic messages through interpreting, exemplifying, classifying, summarizing, inferring, comparing, and explaining.
- Apply. Carrying out or using a procedure for executing or implementing.
- Analyze. Breaking material into constituent parts and determining how the parts relate to one another and to an overall structure or purpose through differentiating, organizing, and attributing.

- Evaluate. Making judgments based on criteria and standards through checking and critiquing.
- Create. Putting elements together to form a coherent or functional whole; reorganizing elements into a new pattern or structure through generating, planning, or producing.

Once you hit the top level of "create," then you can be considered to have a deep grasp on a subject. Without advancing through each level of the taxonomy, you can't adequately perform the next levels. We see this illustrated in our lives every day whenever someone who doesn't have an adequate understanding of a topic seeks to evaluate it and make a judgment upon it. That's because of a failure to follow the taxonomy!

Bloom's taxonomy is a particularly useful tool to help guide and shape your learning process. Basically, the taxonomy is a list of *how* to actively interact with new information. It focuses on the mental processes that allow you to frame information and analyze it, each verb a kind of mental tool to grasp and manipulate new incoming data. Bloom's framework is great because it's so versatile and can be used literally anywhere. In the classroom, at work, or in designing your own systems for achieving your personal goals, this taxonomy gives you a shorthand to work with.

The entire taxonomy is predicated on the mental process of learning, which can actually be summed up quite nicely. Before you can **understand** a concept, you must **remember** it. To **apply** a concept, you must first **understand** it. In order to **evaluate** a process, you must have **analyzed** it. To **create** an accurate conclusion, you must have completed a thorough **evaluation**. The challenge is introspection and understanding where you currently fall on the taxonomy, because only then can you understand what is required for you to move forward in your mastery.

Let's dive into each element more deeply.

First, remembering contains elements like *listening*, *finding* information (using tools like *Googling*, perhaps) actively *memorizing* data, *bookmarking* important information to return to later, *highlighting* key points to synthesize later, and *repeating* information again and again to drill it.

This aspect is all about taking information and fixing it somehow so that you can store it and retrieve it later. If you're the kind of person who likes to make extensive bookmarks and notes about things you want to read or watch later, then you are actively remembering. You are also helping your long-term memory put down information whenever you tabulate or put information in easy-to-remember bullet points. Remembering also entails outlining key features or quotes or defining the main ideas so that you can recall the summary later on. Whenever you revise for an exam, you're using these skills.

Understanding happens whenever we engage with information more actively. Whereas remembering is about concretizing and storing information, understanding is about picking it all apart to better see how it works, like some people do to household appliances! *Categorizing* data (like we're doing here), *grouping* information into chunks, *inferring* from the data you have and *predicting* future events based on it, *summarizing*, and *paraphrasing* in different words are all cognitive operations intended to get to the deeper meaning of a set of symbols or patterns.

Teachers who ask their students to write things "in their own words" are doing so because they don't want to test for memorization; they want to test for understanding. If you comprehend a thing deeply, you are able to manipulate it, no matter how its components are rearranged or what symbols are used to express it. If you've ever tried to explain something complicated to someone who's not familiar with the concept, you may have found it helpful to give them a related example. You could outline a metaphor from a concept that they'd understand more easily and show how the ideas relate to one another. This *relating*, and *associating*, is key to developing deep understanding of a topic.

Applying is the third category. This is, broadly, where information is brought into the "real world" and made manifest, whether that's by *executing*, *sketching*, *acting out*, or *articulating*. As you're probably noticing, many of these terms have significant overlap with other verbs in other categories—and this should obviously be the case, when you consider that the brain isn't ever really performing discrete activities, but rather flowing in one continuous action that, for our purposes, we're trying to understand using different models.

In fact, Bloom's verb taxonomy is itself a form of "applying"—it's *charting* or *presenting* information in a concrete way— i.e., applying the abstract concepts to make manifest a model, idea, or concept. *Painting*, *preparing*, *displaying*, *reenacting*, and even *playing* are all verbs associated with this category of the taxonomy. Every time you make a pie chart to illustrate data, turn a plan into reality, or design an experiment that actually gets carried out, you're "applying."

The fourth category is *analyzing*, which is pretty self-explanatory. Verbs in this category include *questioning*, *explaining*, *organizing, deconstructing, correlating*, and *calculating*. This includes all those verbs that show us actively operating on and manipulating information that comes in, not just to pass it from one form to another, but to look really closely at its constituents, trying to understand them. Bloom's theory itself is an example of *appraising* and *categorizing*. You're participating in these functions when you draw a mind map, integrate one set of ideas with another set, break down a machine into its components, or ask, "Why is this happening?"

The fifth element is *evaluating*, and it includes any verbs that show that we're applying some value judgments to the material in front of us. In the previous category, analysis is value-neutral and merely about understanding. This category, however, concerns things like *criticizing*, *rating*, *reflecting, reviewing*, *assessing*, and *validating*. This is where our brains practice discernment—and the weighing up of the information against stated aims and goals.

How useful are the results of your experiment? What is the quality and veracity of the claims you're appraising? How well did you perform? How can you *editorialize* or else compile all this information into a whole that actually says something?

The final verb group is *creating*. Here, our relationship to information is quite fundamental: we make it! *Composing* music, *mixing* known things to create something new, *filming* a movie, *writing* the script, and *role-playing* the characters are all creative ways to engage with information and build something novel. Other creative endeavors you might not have thought of include *programming*, *designing* systems, *adapting* material from one form into another, or even things like *podcasting* or *blogging*. Curiously, Bloom even considered *leading* to be creative, since leadership often involves guiding people toward an entirely new and self-made vision.

Again, these verbs and categories will always overlap—the point is not to identify discrete categories. Rather, this model is a tool to help you play with information and see it from many different angles, in the same way as a toolbox of differently colored glasses could be worn to look at the same information in different lights. When you're trying to learn and memorize, it makes a huge difference to engage actively and deliberately with information—not just in one or two ways, but in as many as possible. This way, data comes alive, becoming three-dimensional and allowing you a depth of understanding that will last longer than more shallow impressions.

Whenever you're learning something new, you might, for example, highlight the text in the book so you can summarize it (remembering) and then paraphrase that text in your own words (understanding). You can then apply your understanding by constructing your own chart or diagram (applying) and taking some time to break that diagram down, questioning it, and linking it to other diagrams you've already made (analyzing). You can ask yourself after all this whether these methods are actually helping you retain the material (evaluating) and use your assessment to guide the further development of improved systems of learning (creating).

It sounds tedious, and it can be, but that's the true path to information synthesis. In fact, it's this tough mental work and struggle that really cements concepts and facts in your brain.

The SQ3R Method

Next, we come to the SQ3R method, which is excellent for starting from ground zero. You'll have texts or other resources, and you should arrange the best way to approach them from the beginning. This lets you know what you are going to learn, helps you learn it, and then reminds you of what you just learned. This seemingly rudimentary process is invaluable in the synthesis phase.

Textbooks, for instance, are dense, detailed, heavily annotated, and long. It's easy to conjure up the image of a student late at night, glossing over page 349 of a giant volume, growing fatigued and unable to retain the words they're reading the next morning.

That's why American educator Francis P. Robinson developed a method meant to help students really get the most comprehension from the texts they're assigned—and, ergo, the subject they're studying. Robinson sought a way to make reading more active, helping readers by creating dynamic engagement with books so the information stuck in their minds.

The traditional classroom setting of reading and regurgitating certainly isn't the most effective, but it's the only model most of us know. Robinson's approach is suitable for more than just reading: your entire study plan can be modeled on Robinson's method and adapted to your learning.

The technique is called the SQ3R method, named for its five components:

- survey
- question
- read

- recite
- review

Survey. The first step in the method is getting a general overview of what you'll be reading. Textbooks and nonfiction works aren't like fiction or narrative literature, in which you just start from the beginning and wind your way through each chapter. The best works of nonfiction are arranged to impart information in a way that's clear and memorable and builds upon each previous chapter. If you go dive in without surveying first, you are going in blind without understanding where you are going and what you are trying to accomplish. You should get a lay of the land first, *before* you delve into Chapter 1. The survey component is for you to get the most general introduction to the topic so you can establish and shape the goals you want to achieve from reading the book.

It's just like taking a look at the entire map before you set off on a road trip. You may not need all the knowledge at the moment, but understanding everything as a whole and how it fits together will help you with the small details and when you're in the weeds. You'll know that you generally need to head southwest if you're confused.

In the SQ3R method, surveying means examining the structure of the work: the book title, the introduction or preface, section titles, chapter titles, and headings and subheadings. If the book is illustrated with pictures or graphics, you'd review them. You could also make note of the conventions the book uses to guide your reading: typefaces, bold or italic text, and chapter objectives and study questions if they're in there. In using the survey step, you're setting up expectations for what you're going to be reading about and giving yourself an initial framework to structure your goals for reading the material.

For example, let's say you're reading a book to learn more about geology. I happen to have one called *Geology Illustrated* by John S. Shelton—it's about 50 years old and no longer in print, but it works fine for our purposes.

There's a preface describing what's in the book and how the illustrations are arranged. There's an unusually extensive table of contents divided into parts: "Materials," "Structure," "Sculpture," "Time," "Case Histories," and "Implications." That tells me that the book will start with concrete (excuse the pun) geological elements, will flow into how they form over time, important incidents, and what we might expect in the future. That's a pretty good guess at the arc of the book.

Each part is then divided into chapters, which are further divided into a ton of headings and subheadings—too many to mention here, but they give a more nuanced summary of what each part will go into. When you survey and know the significance of what you're currently learning, you are able to instantly comprehend it better. It's the difference between looking at a single gear in isolation versus seeing where and how it works in a complex clock.

Beyond books, you should survey all the important concepts in a discipline. If you can't find it within a structure like a book's table of contents, then you need to be able to create it for yourself. Yes, this is the difficult part, but once you are able to lay all the concepts out and understand how they relate to each other at least on a surface level, you will already be leaps ahead of others. Use the survey component to form an outline of what you'll learn. In a sense, it's more like you're plotting out a metaphorical "book" for yourself.

You want to form a general outline of what you're going to learn. Since you're studying this on your own, there might be a few gaps in what you think you'll need to know. So in this phase, you'll want to determine exactly what you *want* to become knowledgeable about, as specifically as you can make it. For example, if you want to learn all about psychology, that's going to take a significant amount of time. It won't happen in one shot. You'd want to specify it a little more: the early history of psychoanalysis, the works of Sigmund Freud and Carl Jung, sports psychology, developmental psychology—the possibilities are plenty.

You'll want to keep an eye out for phrases or concepts that appear in several different sources, since they represent elements that come up often in your chosen field and might be things you have to know. Draw connections and cause-and-effect relationships before even diving into any of the concepts in detail.

For example, let's say you want to study the history of European cinema. Entering "European cinema history" into Google brings up a lot of interesting possibilities, and some of those can be used to form the outline you want.

You can look for reading materials on Amazon.com, finding the ones that seem the most authoritative. The Internet Movie Database (IMDB) can help you find the most important European films for you to watch. You can discover which European directors are the most cited and appear to be the most important and influential. You can research which European movies are the highest-rated and why. You can collect a few resources on what specific countries had what cinematic movements and why.

Then you'll organize these resources. You'll come up with a plan to study each one—perhaps study a chapter in a book on early European film history, then watch a couple of films that represent the era you're on at the moment and give yourself a film review assignment afterward. Focus on gathering and organizing; you don't need to touch them yet. The important aspect is that you've surveyed the topic before diving in and thus understand what you're getting into and why.

Question. In the second stage of the SQ3R method, you're still not diving into the deep end. During the question stage, you'll work a little more deeply to get your mind more prepared to focus and interact with the material you're reading. You'll take a slightly closer look at the structure of the book and form some questions you wanted answered or set up the objectives you want to achieve.

In the question phase of reading a book—or, more precisely at this point, *preparing* to read—you'd go through the chapter titles, headings, and subheadings and rephrase them in the form of a question. This turns the dry title the author has given into a challenge or problem for you to solve. For example, if you're reading a book on Freud, there might be a chapter called "Foundations of Freud's Analyses of Dreams." You'd rewrite this chapter title as "How did Sigmund Freud's work on dream interpretation originate and what were his very first ideas on the subject?" You could pencil that question in the margin of your book. If you're reading a textbook with study questions at the ends of the chapters, those serve as excellent guides to what you're about to find out.

In the geology book, I'm afraid there aren't too many chapter titles that I could rephrase as inquiries. ("Weathering," "Groundwater," "Glaciation"—that's about it.) But there are headings that might work: "Some Effects of Metamorphism on Sedimentary Rocks," for example, can become "What can happen to bottom-centered rocks through eons of environmental change?" Not only have I changed it to a question, but I've paraphrased the title into wording that I can understand even before I've started reading.

Now that you've organized your resources for study planning, you can arrange some of the topics you're going to cover into questions you want answered or objectives that you want to meet. Based on the source material you've lined up and the patterns that you might have observed, what specific answers are you hoping to find in your studies? Write them down. This is also a good time to come up with a structure for answering your questions—a daily journal, a self-administered quiz, some kind of "knowledge tracker." You don't have to answer the questions yet—you just need to know how you're going to record them when you do.

In our European film history example, if you've done even the most cursory investigation in the survey phase, you undoubtedly came across some directors' names more than once: Federico Fellini, Jean-Luc Godard, Luis Buñuel, Fritz Lang, and so forth. You figure they're going to be important people to get to know, so you could ask the question, "Why was Fellini so influential?" "What was Buñuel's directing style?" "What themes did Godard pursue in his filmmaking?" You might have come across certain concepts or themes that seemed common in European film—"French New Wave," "World War II," "neo-realism," for example. Put these down as targets for your study and arrange them into your outline.

Reading. In this stage you're finally ready to dive into the material. Because you've gotten the lay of the land and formed some questions and goals for your studies, you're a little more engaged when you finally sit down to read. You're looking for answers to the questions you've raised. Another underrated aspect of formulating and organizing before you actually begin reading is to build *anticipation* for learning. You've been looking over everything for a while now, and you'll probably be eager to finally dive in and answer the questions you've been mentally accumulating.

This step is where most people try to start but fail because they lack a foundation and instead have unreasonable expectations.

Now you're being deliberate and paced about your reading so you can comprehend better. This means slowing down—a *lot.* Be patient with the material and with yourself. If a passage is difficult to understand, read it extremely slowly. If you aren't getting a sense of clarity about a certain part, stop, go back to the beginning, and reread it. It's not like you're reading a page-turner novel that you can't put down. You're reading information that might be densely packed—so read it slowly and attentively, one section at a time.

Chances are that reading is part of your study plan, but so might visual aids, online courses, and Internet resources. Use them exactly the way you'd use the book in the reading phase: deliberately and persistently, with the goal of fully understanding each concept you're being taught. If you get lost, remember the rewind button and scrolling are your best buddies. Plan your study time around getting as complete a level of comprehensiveness as you can.

With our European film history example, this is obvious. Watch your films with a critical eye. At certain points you might want to rewind to catch visual images, dialogue, or action that might be pertinent. If you can watch a video with a director's commentary audio track, you'll want to spend an afternoon with that. Cross-check the movies with the books you're reading or the online courses you're taking to answer any questions or lines of thought that you might have.

Reciting. This step is crucial in processing the information you're learning about and is the biggest difference between reading to learn and reading for entertainment. Now that you're familiar with the material, the aim of the reciting phase is to reorient your mind and attention to focus and learn more fully as you go along. In other words, this step is about literal recitation.

Ask questions—out loud, verbally—about what you're reading. This is also the point where you take copious notes in the margins of the text and underline or highlight key points. Recitation is verbal and also through writing. However, it's important to restate these points *in your own words* rather than just copy phrases from the book onto a piece of paper. By doing this, you're taking the new knowledge and putting it into phrases of which you already know the meaning. This makes the information easier to grasp in a language you understand. It makes it significant and meaningful to you.

My geology book happens to have pretty wide margins on the sides of the pages, so I have some nice room to rephrase and rewrite key points as well as highlight important concepts. For example, consider the following original text:

> This comparison suggests that the slow progress of erosion on hills and mountains is similar to the much more rapid and observable changes seen in miniature all about us.

I could rewrite the above into something like this:

Mountains and hills experience the same decay as happens in lowlands and rivers, just more slowly. Similar to baseball players.

What I'm doing here is putting one single bit of information into two distinct phrases, one of which I had to come up with myself. This is a huge tool that's used in memorization, and it's also a great way to make the information more meaningful to me personally. I also added a bit about baseball because I like baseball, and it makes the concept instantly understandable when I look back at it. Repeated throughout the course of a whole book, this process multiplies your learning capacity by itself.

The recitation phase in organizing your studies is great because it works across different mediums, and there are plenty of ways you can express your questions and restatements.

Going back to our European cinema example, if you're watching Ingmar Bergman's *The Seventh Seal* (short summary: medieval knight meets angel of death, tries to buy time by playing chess with him), you might write down questions about its Biblical references, the art direction, the Middle Ages references, or the cinematography. You could also write a summary or do a video blog of the movie and address the key sequences that are most relevant to your questions. You could also compare it to other films by Bergman or note similarities his style has with other directors that you're studying. The important part is that you are taking the time to rephrase and recite new knowledge and make it meaningful to you—and no one else.

Review. The final stage of the SQ3R plan is when you go back over the material that you've studied, re-familiarize yourself with the most important points, and build your skills at memorizing the material.

Robinson breaks this stage down into specific days of the week, but we'll just mention some of the tactics in general. They include writing more questions about important parts you have highlighted, orally answering some of the questions if you can, reviewing your notes, creating flashcards for important concepts and terminology, rewriting the table of contents using your own words, and building out a mind map. Any kind of practice that helps you drill down, take in, and commit information to memory is fair game (though flashcards are especially effective).

This step is meant to strengthen your memory of the material, but it does more than that. It can help you see connections and similarities between different aspects that you might not have picked up at first and put concepts and ideas into greater context. It can also improve your mental organization skills so you can use this practice for other topics.

Think of this step as the natural continuation of the survey step. At this point, you've gained an outline of the field, you've gotten into the nitty-gritty, and now you should take a step back, reevaluate, and make updated, more accurate, and insightful connections. Pair that with memorization and your path to self-learning and expertise becomes essentially a shortcut.

My geology book has no shortage of terms that I could put onto flashcards. "Monocline," "stratification," "glacial scour"—whip out the Sharpie now. But I could also map out the process of glaciation in a flowchart or some other visual medium. I could make a timeline of the ages of the earth and link it with the most significant geological changes that took place during each era. I can also take down questions that come up that the book either left unanswered or made me want to investigate more fully.

You can use most elements of the book review phase for study planning in the same way. In our European cinema example, you could make a catalog or database for European film directors that outlines their work, their main themes, or their stylistic choices. You can draw up flashcards that will help you recall the important facets of different European strains: "neo-realism," "giallo horror," "spaghetti Western," and "cinéma du look."

And of course you can journal what you've learned, either in written form or some visual expression.

The SQ3R method is no joke. It's exhaustive and detailed and will take patience and sharp organization to pull off. But if you give yourself the patience and devotion to take each step seriously and slowly, you'll find it incredibly helpful to tackle a complex subject. And each time you do it, it's a little easier than the last.

Finally, we come to self-explanation and the art of self-torture as a means to deeper understanding and comprehension.

Self-Explanation

Self-explanation sounds simple, but there is a method to the simplicity. It's more than merely thinking out loud. It involves explaining and articulating information to establish a baseline of knowledge and blind spots.

Blind spots are when we don't realize what we don't know. But with self-explanation, you will quickly learn what you don't understand, and it might be far more than you expected. Here's how it can sometimes show itself in real life.

If you've been around small children under age seven or so, you may have witnessed (or experienced, if you're a parent) a phenomenon we call "the why chain." This is when kids ask an initial question about the world—say, "Where does rain come from?"—and, after hearing our answer ("From clouds"), continue down a path of relentless questions to get at a definitive, ending answer ("Why don't the clouds hold in the rain?" "Why can't the clouds just fall to the earth still shaped like clouds?" "Why don't the clouds on a sunny day let rain go?").

Yes, this line of questioning can be a recipe for tedium. But it's reflective of a child's innate capacity for endless curiosity for a definitive answer. (For parents, of course, this point usually comes a lot earlier.)

Elaborative interrogation has something in common with that childlike inquiry, except it relates to more advanced topics that adults are (hopefully) liable to investigate.

Simply put, elaborative interrogation is an effort to create explanations for *why* stated facts are true. This is what drives home comprehension, as well as what you *don't* comprehend.

In elaborative interrogation, the learner inquires about how and why certain concepts work. Nothing is safe from this inquiry. They go through their study materials to determine the answers and try to find connections between all the ideas they're learning about. Can you answer simple questions or at least understand what the answer is likely to be?

"Why" questions are more significant than "what" questions, which primarily relate to the natures of identification and memorization. A linc of "why" questions elicits a better understanding of the factors and reasons for a given subject. We can memorize all the parts of a flower—the petal, the stamen, the pistil, the receptacle, and so on—but the names alone mean nothing to us. We have to ask what each part of a flower does and why that role is integral to its lifespan.

This method is effective because it's simple and anyone can apply it easily. Elaborative interrogation does, however, require some existing knowledge about the topic to generate solid questions for yourself.

Elaborative interrogation could proceed like this, and suppose you are learning about the Great Depression of the 1930s:

- The first thing you'd ask would be, well, **what was it?** It was the biggest worldwide economic breakdown in the history of the industrialized world.

- **What caused the Great Depression?** A few key events, like the stock market crash of October 1929, the failure of over 9,000 banks, declines in consumer spending, high tax on imports from Europe, and drought conditions in the agricultural sector.

- Let's talk about the stock market crash. **Why did it happen?** Some experts were concerned about margin-selling, declines in the British stock market, out-of-control speculation, and some questionable business practices in the steel industry.

- ***Margin-selling? What was that? How did margin-selling work, and why was it a problem?*** Margin-selling (or margin-trading) is when an investor borrows money from a broker to buy stock. So many investors used it that most stock purchases were bought with this borrowed money. It worked so well that the stock prices went up—and when the asset bubble popped, prices fell off. Since the investor had no funds to repay the loan, both the broker and the investor had no profit to show for it.

And the chain of interrogation goes on from there. You use your study materials to obtain the answers to the "why" and "how" questions. Once you've sufficiently established those answers, you go back to the other aspects of the Great Depression and the stock market crash and determine how each aspect related to one another. *How did margin-selling affect the banks? How did margin-selling relate to the decline in consumer spending? Did the drought affect the trade issues with Europe?*

The overall point of elaborative interrogation is to make sure there are no holes in your understanding. If you can survive your own questioning, it's likely you can survive tests, exams, and when other people ask you to teach them. You can start with the journalistic questions (who, what, where, when, why, how), then move on to contextual questions (how did this happen and what happens after) for a good, thorough start to understanding.

The range of topics for which you can use elaborative interrogation is practically limitless. For example, math students can use it to break down advanced calculations and establish patterns that might help in higher-level math topics. If you're studying human biology, you can use the technique to determine the specific conditions that lead to medical conditions like high cholesterol or heart arrhythmia. Even students of literature can use the technique to study motifs, trends, and themes in a particular author's work.

Elaborative interrogation, when you think about it, is a form of self-explanation. You are quizzing yourself and then putting yourself on the spot as to whether you can answer or not. You should be able to see how this lets you know where you lack comprehension and facts. Having knowledge is of course important to learning, but sometimes not having blind spots is just as important.

The Feynman Technique

Elaborative interrogation is one method of asking yourself questions that focuses on you seeing the whole picture behind a piece of information. You can use the journalistic questions or contextual and background questions.

The Feynman technique, named for Nobel Prize–winning physicist Richard Feynman, is another type of discussing with yourself. Known as the "Great Explainer," Feynman was revered for his ability to clearly illustrate dense topics like quantum physics for virtually anybody. In *Feynman's Lost Lecture: The Motion of Planets Around the Sun*, David Goodstein writes that Feynman prided himself on being able to explain the most complex ideas in the simplest terms. It stemmed from his own study techniques as a student at Princeton University, and he refined the method as a professor and teacher of physics.

Most of us have internal monologues in some form or another throughout most of the day. Verbalizing these conversations in the context of problem-solving spurs more cognizant attention to how your mind works through a problem.

Properly carried out, the Feynman technique will prove whether you really understand a topic or have glossed over certain important concepts. It's also suitable for almost every conceivable subject, allowing you to see the gaps in your knowledge that need to be connected.

If you feel your explanations are long, rambling, or protracted, you may not have grasped the subject as well as you may have thought.

The usefulness of the Feynman technique is especially helpful in scientific or technological topics, but it's adaptable for any subject. Literature students can use it to narrow down themes, historians can use it to explain events and historical patterns, and civics students can use it to understand living conditions or urban issues—there's really no restriction on how you can use it. All you need to do is honestly answer the questions you are asking yourself, and you will quickly see where you need to focus your attention.

The Feynman technique is a specific application of elaborative interrogation. Remember, the goal is not to actually answer the questions; it's to see what you are *unable* to answer—that is the information it provides. It has four steps.

Step One: Choose your concept.

The Feynman technique is very widely applicable, so let's choose one example we can use throughout this section: gravity. Suppose that we want to either understand the basics about gravity or explain it to someone else. This can obviously differ depending on what you are learning at the moment.

Step Two: Write down an explanation of the concept in plain English.

Can you do it? Is this easy or difficult? This is the truly important step because it will show exactly what you do and do not understand about the concept of gravity. Explain it as simply, yet accurately, as you can and in a way that someone who knows nothing about the concept would also understand.

So going back to the concept we are using, how would *you* define gravity? Would it be something about being attracted to large masses? Would it be something that makes us fall? Or would it be about how our planet was formed? Can you do it, or will you resort to saying, "Well, you know… it's gravity!"

This step allows you to see your blind spots and where your explanation starts to fall apart. If you can't perform this step, clearly you don't know as much about it as you thought, and you would be terrible at explaining it to someone else.

You might be able to explain what happens to objects that are subject to gravity and what happens when there is zero gravity. You might also be able to explain the causes of gravity. But everything that happens in between might be something you assume you know but continually skip learning about.

Step Three: Find your blind spots.

If you were unable to come up with a short description of gravity in the previous step, then it's clear you have large gaps in your knowledge. Research gravity and find a way to describe it in a simple way. You might come up with something like "The force that causes larger objects to attract smaller objects because of their weight and mass." Whatever you are unable to explain, this is a blind spot you must rectify.

Being able to analyze information and break it down in a simple way demonstrates knowledge and understanding. If you can't summarize it in one sentence, or at least in a brief and concise manner, you still have blind spots you need to learn about. This technique is how you can find them easily and make sure you understand the concepts you are taking notes on and learning. I encourage you to take a second and try this right now. What seemingly simple concept can you try to explain? Can you actually do it, or does it reveal a lack of understanding somewhere in the process?

Step Four: Use an analogy.

Finally, create an analogy for the concept. What is the purpose of this step? It's an extension of step three. Making analogies between concepts requires an understanding of the main traits and characteristics of each. This step is to demonstrate whether or not you truly understand it on a deeper level and to make it easier to explain. You can look at it as the true test of your understanding and whether you still possess blind spots in your knowledge.

For example, gravity is like when you put your foot into a pool and the fallen leaves on the surface are attracted to it because it causes a barely seen impact. That impact is gravity.

This step also connects new information to old information and lets you piggyback off a working mental model to understand or explain in greater depth. Of course, it's unlikely that you can do step four if you can't do steps two and three, but sometimes you can do steps two and three and find you can't do step four—now you understand the boundaries of your knowledge better.

The Feynman technique is a rapid way to discover what you know versus what you think you know, and it allows you to solidify your knowledge base. When you keep explaining and simplifying to yourself and discover that you can't, you've just discovered that you don't know as much as you thought you did.

Remember, it's another extension of elaborative interrogation, which is where you quiz yourself by asking questions where you can demonstrate your comprehension or lack thereof. Tedium is indeed the name of the game in this phase, but your brain will feel no motivation to learn, progress, or grow without it.

Takeaways:

- Information synthesis is the second branch of effective learning in a way that our brain likes. Synthesis, or comprehension and understanding by other names, is probably the true bedrock of what we would usually consider learning. It's taking on a new concept or set of information and knowing it inside and out. It's knowing the context it fits in and seeing it from as many angles as possible to ensure that understanding is true and thorough, especially with regard to blind spots.

That sounds like a tall order, and it is. But it's this very struggle and slog that cements understanding and retention. It's not necessarily "no pain, no gain" but the brain simply sees no reason to remember something if there is no apparent reason to (i.e., it is not forced to work for it).

- Bloom's taxonomy is a wonderful tool for understanding and manipulating information. It's a sequence of thought elements that go into deep synthesis. In fact, each of the six phases imparts a guideline for how to interact with information more deeply to ensure comprehension. Before you can understand a concept, you must remember it. To apply a concept, you must first understand it. In order to evaluate a process, you must have analyzed it. To create an accurate conclusion, you must have completed a thorough evaluation. The challenge is introspection and understanding where you currently fall on the taxonomy, because only then can you understand

what is required for you to move forward in your understanding.
- The SQ3R method is another tool for better understanding. It's about interacting with the resources you use for learning. Where most people may read or listen to something once and call it a day, the SQ3R stands for survey, question, read, recite, and review. That's roughly five layers of analysis for you to grow your understanding. We learn better when we know what's ahead and when we know what just occurred.
- Self-explanation (elaborative interrogation) and the Feynman technique are the final tools for better information synthesis. When we are forced to try to explain concepts through self-inquiry, we will quickly discover what we do know and what we don't know at all. These are called blind spots, and they are far more common than you might like to think. Can you explain why the sky is blue or how gravity works? Probably not off the top of your head, even though you think you understand those concepts. The Feynman technique

is an offshoot of self-explanation that helps find blind spots as well, with an added component of using an analogy to explain what you think you know. This is probably the most powerful tool because it instantly makes you feel ignorant—a positive thing in the realm of learning.

Chapter 4. Information Retention

We now arrive at the third and final pillar of learning, which is retaining the information you've absorbed and processed. We've seen that when it comes to processing and analyzing (the previous pillar), the brain has an almost endless array of functions and different ways to play and engage with information once it's been absorbed. This chapter is about how all of this data is inserted into your long-term memory banks and *kept* there. Though the manipulation and analysis of information is usually what we think of when we hear the word "thinking," the truth is that none of it will amount to much if you can't *actively* store this information and have access to it later.

You can reach into your memory banks, but it doesn't matter if they are empty.

Make It Emotional

We've briefly alluded to it in previous chapters in a negative sense, but an excellent way to make information stand out in the mind is to *make it emotional.* To distinguish from the problems the limbic system can create, emotion is helpful when it is an *association*, but not when it overtakes the brain.

You probably don't need any evidence for this to know it's true. Wasn't it always the juiciest, most bizarre, or most personally relevant details from your school curriculum that you remembered most? Which news story do you pay more attention to and remember later: the shocking and emotionally charged one about your alma mater or the boring one about interest rates in Tanzania?

The stronger the emotion aroused, the greater the effect, although it goes without saying that you don't want to traumatize yourself with associations that are too stressful or depressing! Doing so could have the opposite effect—i.e., you kick your brain into fight-or-flight mode and immediately compromise your ability to learn and retain.

Because of the way we've evolved, our brains will always prioritize emotional material like fear and anger (or lust, for that matter), since it's these emotions that are most closely linked to survival. And since, as we've seen, the emotional limbic brain plays such a crucial role in memory and learning, we can use emotions to our advantage.

There are two main ways to do this: (1) by associating new information to something significant in your personal life (i.e., to material already in your long-term memory) or (2) by assigning emotions to new information.

As to the first method, this occurs when we actively create a connection to an existing memory, exemplified by the phrase, "This reminds me of when…"

As for the second method, neuroscientists have discovered that our emotional state at the moment we make a new memory affects how efficiently we encode and memorize it. Not only this, but the emotion itself can sometimes serve as a "hook" to retrieve the memory later. In the same way that being in the same room you were in when you first learned a fact helps you remember that same fact, being in the same state of mind in which you absorbed new information can help you access that information again more easily. This is all to say that if you were in the habit of learning the capitals of European countries when you were in an angry state, then being in an angry state would help you recall those capitals.

Our brain is busy making associations, and anything associated with a strong emotion will also become charged and easier to remember. We can remember more vividly when the absorption phase happened during mind states of excitement, fear, or anger.

The *Stroop test* is an experiment that shows this effect in action. Participants are presented with words in quick succession, with each printed in a different color, and asked to say the name of this color. Later, they were also asked to recall as many of the words they'd seen as possible. As you can imagine, the few taboo words that had been thrown in were far more likely to be remembered than more neutral words, presumably because of the strong emotional reaction they elicited. This is evidence for the first principle we outlined above, namely that assigning strong emotion to a stimulus means the stimulus is better encoded, consolidated, and recalled from memory banks.

On the other hand, a Harvard paper published in 1977 explored the phenomenon of "lightbulb memories." Do you remember exactly what you were doing during September 11, 2001? Though it might have been something pretty mundane, the fact that it was tied to a momentous, meaningful event means it comes along for the ride, as though the strong emotion was a bright spotlight that temporarily illuminated the information around you for that moment, making you able to recall the details vividly. These are lightbulb memories, and they're so powerful because they're associated with events that are personally significant to us. Again, our emotional state at the time of an event affects how well we encode it as memory.

Importantly, this is not to say that objectively "important" events will be more readily remembered, only that these events are likely to stir up strong personal associations and emotions, and it's these that ensure a memory is firmly embedded in the brain. For those who aren't American, or those who weren't as deeply shocked by the September 11 events, their lightbulb memories may be less pronounced.

It's easy to see why all of this should be the way it is. As we've already explored in previous chapters, the "higher" thinking brain occupies a relatively minor percentage of our total brainpower, with most of it going to more emotional processing. Again, there is an evolutionary advantage to being able to recall more emotionally charged events, and this is likely a trait we've inherited from our ancestors. Emotions act extremely quickly, far more quickly than the processes of our rational, conscious, thinking brain, and this is extremely useful in situations where we need to act swiftly to protect ourselves.

Negative emotions are there, in other words, to keep us safe, and the fact that we prioritize them cognitively in the present means that at some point in the past it served our ancestors to do so. Keeping out of physical harm's way is always going to be more pressing than developing those skills needed to remember the possibly boring details for an exam. Still, you can make use of the mental machinery you have by making that boring material a little less boring so you remember it more easily.

A 2007 study by researcher Harald Schupp showed that people paid more attention to images showing injuries (i.e., more emotionally charged images) than neutral ones. Unsurprisingly, it seems that our attention is more keenly drawn to emotive subjects and held there for longer. This suggests that we make better memories where strong emotions are involved because those emotions help us sit up and pay attention, which in turn boosts absorption and enhances our memory.

An interesting and related phenomenon is "attentional blink"—which is the brief moment where we are unable to focus on a second stimulus after switching attention from another subject. This means we may be less able to remember something if we've been intensely focusing on something else the moment before. This effect seems even more pronounced when the thing being focused on is very emotional in nature. Someone might experience a very traumatic car crash, and in that moment, heightened awareness and attention helped them put down incredibly vivid memories of every detail of the crash, almost as though it played out in slow motion. However, that person may also report that they went a little "blank" the few moments after the crash and don't really remember any details of what happened next.

A 1981 study by Gordon Bower showed that people can better remember information that closely matches their mood at the time they encoded the information. Someone may really remember an unhappy character and the details of their story if, when they read about them, they felt similarly unhappy. They might more easily forget the details of other happy characters they encountered during that time. You may find yourself identifying more with different actors in a movie depending on your mood. It turns out that your ability to remember these people is also affected.

This is called the *mood congruence effect.* Emotions are understood to affect both the storage and retrieval of information, mediated by the hippocampus and the amygdala in the limbic brain. You can more easily retrieve a memory if your emotional state matches the state you were in when you made the memory.

So how can you use all this information to help you learn better and retain what you memorize? The first step is to understand that learning is not a dull, neutral activity that happens somewhere in lofty, rational parts of our brain that are unconnected to the rest of our experience. Emotions play an important, if not the most important, role in memory creation and retrieval. So as you study or learn something new, keep this in mind.

Try to connect new information with information already stored in your memory banks, and the more emotional, the better. You are more likely to remember the details of a complex chemical equation if you've assigned each molecule the role of one of your family members and tell yourself an emotionally compelling story about how they gain and lose carbon atoms in a big family argument. Imagine the players in a history textbook all belong to different houses from *Game of Thrones*, or use rude or humorous mnemonics to help you remember boring programming acronyms. Liberally sprinkle your study notes with names of people who mean something to you, ideas and themes from your life, current affairs, or pop culture references that will stick in your memory. If a new anatomical process seems alien to you, rewrite it in your mind as a cake recipe (if you're an avid baker) or a cheesy soap opera from your childhood.

You can also simply try to imbue the things you're learning with emotion, even if it doesn't connect directly to old memories. A string of boring words is easier to remember if you make up a little story that links them all together, particularly if the story is a gruesome horror tale. Simply taking the effort to make this story is already giving you a head start to recalling it better later on.

Don't try and force dry, irrelevant information into your mind. In reality, all information is neutral, and it's up to your perception to make it fascinating or emotional. Put it into a form that appeals to you, however specific, bizarre, taboo, or sad that may be. When you try to recall that information, temporarily feel that emotion again and you'll be amazed at how swiftly you can access those memories again. Have you ever noticed how certain smells can take you right back to highly specific emotional moments in your past? This is because the neurons responsible for smell are particularly associated with the emotional limbic center.

You can use any of the techniques and methods we've described above combined with the power of emotion to boost your learning and memory capacity. Study each new chapter in a new room in your house, and tie the material to real lived memories you've had in each of those rooms; the more emotional, the better. Use smells, touch, taste, or sound to add texture to your memories.

Turn the information over in your mind as you process it, trying on as many of Bloom's taxonomy verbs as possible. Use visual, auditory, tactile, or kinetic information, and *tell stories* to add in that crucial emotional element. When you use chunking to condense information and reduce your cognitive load, chunk according to emotion. Simplify complex tasks by turning them into silly rhymes or games, childhood memories, or ideas that get you riled up. Once your limbic system has helped you retrieve that memory, your "higher" brain can kick in and fill in the more neutral, objective details.

We can utilize our brain's tendency to prefer what might generally be called outlier information in another way that we glazed over: constructing vivid imagery.

Along with emotional and outlier information, a large body of research indicates that visual cues help us better retrieve and remember information. The research outcomes on visual learning make complete sense when you consider that our brain is mainly an image processor (much of our sensory cortex is devoted to vision), not a word processor. In fact, the part of the brain used to process words is quite small in comparison to the part that processes visual images.

Words are abstract and rather difficult for the brain to retain, whereas visuals are concrete and, as such, more easily remembered.

There are countless studies that have confirmed the power of visual imagery in learning. For instance, one study asked students to remember many groups of three words each, such as "dog," "bike," and "street." Students who tried to remember the words by repeating them over and over again did poorly on recall. In comparison, students who made the effort to make visual associations with the three words, such as imagining a dog riding a bike down the street, had significantly better recall.

Based upon research outcomes, the effective use of vivid visuals can decrease learning time, improve comprehension, enhance retrieval, and increase retention. Memory is largely visual, so we should take advantage of that.

Take a list of objects you want to memorize: rabbit, coffee, blanket, hair, cactus, running, mountain, tea. There are eight items.

This would seem to be incredibly difficult to memorize because everything is unrelated. However, you can give yourself a better chance by creating a vivid and striking mental image for each item. It doesn't have to be a literal representation of the word or even be related to it.

For instance, what images can you create for "rabbit"? You could use a mental image of a normal, cute rabbit, but that's not likely to be distinctive in your memory. You could conjure up an image of what the word "rabbit" makes you think of, a symbol, what the word sounds like to you, or how the word is written. The more outrageous and unusual, the better for you to memorize, because we tend to easily forget normal things.

When you put this same amount of thought into the eight items of that list, you will be able to memorize them more effectively. It's not just taking advantage of how your brain works; it's the attention and time to choosing an appropriate mental image.

When you can get into the habit of not taking information at face value and going deeper, thinking about it, and constructing vivid imagery to make it stand out in your mind, you'll remember things far better. It might even be the simple act of taking the time and picking out vivid imagery that makes things stick in your brain, but whatever the case, it works.

The next thing we can take to memorize better is to create a vivid story, one that will stand out and make it difficult to forget.

When you can create meaningful connections between items instead of trying to memorize dry facts, you stand a better chance. A story ends up being one large piece of information rather than eight distinct pieces; this is similar to what happens when you attempt to chunk information from earlier in this lesson.

By creating a story for those same eight words, you'll be able to memorize all of them in the correct order far more easily. What kind of story might you construct with the list we have? As with the previous method, the more unusual and outrageous, the better and more memorable it will be.

As a reminder: rabbit, coffee, blanket, hair, cactus, running, mountain, tea.

It could start with a rabbit who went to jail for selling drugs hidden with coffee. He has now tried to attack his cellmates in jail by making weapons with his blanket and hair tied together. However, one day, he found a cactus while running outside in the prison yard. By trading this cactus for three kilograms of tea, he was able to escape to the mountains above the jail and was never seen again.

One item is a brain trigger that helps you remember the next item. It's similar to hearing a song and each verse brings you to remember the next verse and you can remember all the words to a song.

The main principles of this technique are to make each item distinctive (imagination) and link it to the next one (association). The crazier you can make the story, the better. The more distinctive, the more it will stick in your mind. When you make up your story, visualize it in your head with as much color and movement as possible. Practice the story two or three times. Then test yourself to see how many you can remember. Like I've said before, these techniques to improve memory are so effective because they're a reflection of how memory works.

Creating a story is another way to pay close attention to your information and then have it make sense to you in a way that lets you recall it easily. The main idea is to create meaning from meaningless and unrelated facts or information, which of course makes it easier to remember.

Active, Not Passive

Researcher John Dunlosky and his associates conducted a thorough review of techniques and models related to learning in 2013. They examined 10 different methods, chosen because they were "relatively easy to use and hence could be adopted by many students." You'll probably recognize all of them as techniques that you've tried in the past with varying degrees of success.

Dunlosky's team rated each technique according to how well it was suited for the goal of learning and retention. As might be expected, the five models the team thought were *poor* for learning proved to be, arguably, the most commonly used and recognized.

Summarization. In this model, students are asked to write their own summaries of text to be learned. The point of summarization is to "identify the main points of a text and capture the gist of it while excluding unimportant or repetitive material." Dunlosky's team claimed summarization is a skill that only works if the student was already trained in how to do it. For the majority of students *without* that training, the technique couldn't be executed and wouldn't be effective. In other words, this might be effective, and in theory it is, but you are probably doing it wrong.

Highlighting. This long-standing, universally popular technique simply consists of marking pertinent text with a brightly colored ink marker or by underlining. The researchers found that highlighting might help a little if students were using it on an extraordinarily difficult text, but overall, they saw highlighting as a detraction from learning, as it doesn't help students draw additional meaning or inference from the study material.

Mnemonics. A practically ancient practice, mnemonics is the invocation of mental callbacks or shorthand—images, songs, phrases, or acronyms—to recall facts or information already learned—for example, using the phrase "Super Man Helps Every One" to identify the Great Lakes (Superior, Michigan, Huron, Erie, Ontario) or using pictures of objects in learning a foreign language. Researchers found that while it may help us quickly access memory of keywords, the potential of achieving "durable learning" from mnemonics was quite low. This might be connected to what we discussed with the relationship between rote memorization and concept learning.

Imagery use for text learning. A more abstract use of mental invocation than mnemonics, this device encourages students to conjure an image—mentally or on paper—to represent paragraphs or blocks of text they read. The researchers found this use of imagery "promising," although more study on the topic was needed. Overall, they found that the benefits of imagery use were limited to memory tests and text that already lent itself to image creation or memory recall. Note that this is quite different from the vivid, emotional, and story-based imagery we just talked about in the previous section.

Rereading. Dunlosky's team found that although rereading and reviewing text was extremely common and easy to execute, it was only somewhat effective and mainly when rereadings of the text were spaced apart. They also maintained there wasn't compelling evidence that rereading had any effect on students' knowledge, abilities, or deep comprehension of the topic.

While these five techniques weren't without certain advantages—either their ease of use or their effectiveness when students knew how to use them *properly*—Dunlosky found their efficacy in retaining deep understanding, thoroughness, and applicability somewhat narrow and frequently subject to certain conditions. They held some value in superficial meaning or memorization, but far less in comprehension.

What these ineffective methods have in common in fact is the degree of passivity they use. When you attempt to learn something passively, this is tantamount to wishing learning could occur through osmosis: low-effort exposure. You're welcome to try it, but you may quickly realize that nothing was really retained if you're not willing to learn actively, which necessarily involves a degree of struggle and discomfort. Just like the pain of working out and exercising for our physical bodies, this is how our brains advance and progress.

So then, you ask, what did Dunlosky and his team find to be particularly active and effective in learning? There are two methods in particular, and they come next.

Spaced Repetition

Spaced repetition—otherwise known as *distributed practice*—is just what it sounds like.

In order to commit more to memory and retain information better, you space out your rehearsal and exposure to it over as long of a period as possible. In other words, you learn information and skills far better if you study them for one hour each day versus twenty hours in one weekend. Similarly, research has shown that seeing something twenty times in one day is far less effective than seeing something ten times over the course of seven days. *So much for cramming.*

What does this say about how to practice? Spaced repetition is the concept that five minutes a day is far superior to learning and memory than an hour a week. When you focus on *frequency* of learning versus duration or even intensity, you will learn better. Focusing on duration usually becomes motion for motion's sake and can oftentimes become detrimental overall to your goals.

Again, think of the brain as a muscle. Muscles can't be exercised all the time and then put back to work with little to no recovery. Your brain needs time to make connections between concepts, create muscle memory, and generally become familiar with something. Sleep has been shown to be where neural connections are made, and it's not just mental. Synaptic connections are made and dendrites are stimulated in your brain.

If an athlete works out too hard in one session like you might be tempted to do in studying, one of two things will happen. The athlete will either be too exhausted and the latter half of the workout will have been useless, or the athlete will become injured. Rest and recovery are necessary to the task of learning, and sometimes effort isn't what's required.

So when you focus on frequency, suddenly you have a clear structure to organize your practice with. Without a plan in place, most people will just study and practice until their eyes or fingers bleed and they collapse from exhaustion, but that's not working smart, just hard. If you follow what spaced repetition prescribes, you'll have your schedule for optimal learning set up for you.

Let's take studying for a topic you have trouble with: Spanish history. If you have trouble with this topic, that just means even more frequency should be devoted to it. A study or practice schedule focused solely on duration would be relentless from Monday to Sunday. Here's a look at what an optimized schedule focused on frequency might look like.

Monday at 10:00 a.m. Learn initial facts about Spanish history. You accumulate five pages of notes.

Monday at 8:00 p.m. Review notes about Spanish history, but don't just review passively. Make sure to try to recall the information from your own memory. Recalling is a much better way to process information than simply rereading and reviewing. This might only take twenty minutes.

Tuesday at 10:00 a.m. Try to recall the information without looking at your notes much. After you first try to actively recall as much as possible, go back through your notes to see what you missed and make note of what you need to pay closer attention to. This will probably take only fifteen minutes.

Tuesday at 8:00 p.m. Review notes. This will take ten minutes.

Wednesday at 4:00 p.m. Try to independently recall the information again, and only look at your notes once you are done to see what else you have missed. This will take only ten minutes. Make sure not to skip any steps.

Thursday at 6:00 p.m. Review notes. This will take ten minutes.

Friday at 10:00 a.m. Active recall session. This will take ten minutes.

Looking at this schedule, note that you are only studying an additional 75 minutes throughout the week but that you've managed to go through the entire lesson a whopping six additional times. Not only that, you've likely committed most of it to memory because you are using active recall instead of passively reviewing your notes. Even if you take your time to be thorough and double the overall time to 150 minutes, it's still a fraction of what you would have previously spent to do far less.

It's astonishing what you can accomplish in short periods of time if you focus on frequency and don't allow yourself to drift. Scheduling relatively shorter time periods for material keeps you on your toes and prevents you from slipping into laziness if you were to schedule huge blocks of time for one task.

You're ready for a test the next Monday. Actually, you're ready for a test by Friday afternoon. Spaced repetition gives your brain time to process concepts and make its own connections and leaps because of the repetition.

Think about what happens when you have repeated exposure to a concept or skill. For the first couple of exposures, you may not see anything new. As you get more familiar with it and stop going through the motions, you begin to examine it on a deeper level and think about the context surrounding it. You begin to relate it to other concepts or information, and you generally make sense of it below surface level.

There is no mindless motion: it must be active and engaged—which you can only do in short spurts. Flashcards are particularly useful for this, especially if you keep shuffling them and putting them into different orders.

It also helps to pick a different starting spot in the material for each session so you are mixing up the order and aren't just going over the same spots each time. The idea is to keep injecting freshness and different perspectives on the same material that you're seeing multiple times a day.

All of this is designed to push information from your short-term memory into your long-term memory. That's why cramming or studying at the last minute isn't an effective means of learning. Very little tends to make it into long-term memory because of the lack of repetition and deeper analysis. At that point, it becomes rote memorization instead of the concept learning we discussed earlier, which is destined to fade far more quickly.

Hopefully from this point on, instead of measuring the number of hours you spend on something, try instead to measure the number of times you can revisit it. Make it your goal to increase the frequency of reviewing, not necessarily the duration. Ideally you have both, but the literature on spaced repetition makes clear that breathing room is more important.

Spaced repetition generally has two different uses. You can use it for initial learning, but you can also use it to prevent forgetting and to ensure things stick in your brain. The above example was focused on the initial learning phase, but a sample schedule to prevent forgetting and to simply keep things in mind will look a bit lighter. It will strategically touch upon information just enough to keep it in your mind, but not too much as to waste time or hit the point of diminishing returns (which is when you have already memorized it).

For example, Monday: 12:00 p.m., Wednesday: 12:00 p.m., Saturday: 12:00 p.m. Our brains don't necessarily want to remember more than is necessary and will dump information at the first opportunity, so spaced repetition is far superior than one large block of time on one day.

Imagine a path in a garden that gets worn with time. The path is a memory in your brain, and it takes a certain amount of repetitions to become deep enough to stand on its own. Even a few repetitions can make a huge difference as to how clear the path becomes and how long the path will last.

If you're really pressed for time, just know that studying something twice is better than once, almost always. If you want to improve your memory and skill instantly, review something for fifteen minutes before you sleep at the end of your day. That's all it takes to get a head start on others and learn better. Just in case you are looking for a more step-by-step guideline on using spaced repetition and optimizing for frequency, here are four points.

1. Copy my study plan regarding Spanish history. Seven times a week sounds like a lot, but in reality, it ends up only being an extra one to two hours. This helps you keep focused and capitalizes on the way your brain prefers to absorb information. Calibrate your plan to whether you are in the initial learning phase or the "don't forget" phase.

2. Prioritize frequency—at least once a day, but ideally twice a day over the course of a week. Measure in terms of how many times you can get through the material—i.e., repetitions—and not how long you spend on it. Again, calibrate this to whether you are in the learning phase or the "don't forget" phase.

3. Engage with the material each time and don't just go through the motions.

This might require you to create different and creative ways to look at the same thing over and over. As mentioned, you can use different starting points, different flashcards, and overall different ways of reading the same material over and over. Vary the input method here.

4. Test yourself. Don't skip over things and don't just review, read, or recognize. If it feels too easy, you aren't learning optimally.

Self-Testing and Retrieval Practice

Retrieval practice makes us dig deep into our memory banks and work hard mentally, but at the same time, it's one of the most effective ways of truly learning information. It is the third pillar of self-learning.

We typically consider learning as something we absorb—something that goes *into* our brains: the teacher or textbook spits facts, data, equations, and words out at us, and we just sit there and collect them. It's merely accumulation—a very *passive* act.

This kind of relationship with learning returns knowledge that we don't retain for very long because, even though we *get* it, we don't *do* much with it. For best results, we have to make learning an *active* operation.

That's where retrieval practice comes into play. Instead of putting more stuff *into* our brains, retrieval practice helps us take knowledge *out* of our brains and put it to use. That's what cements memory. That seemingly small change in thinking dramatically improves our chances of retaining and remembering what we learn. Everyone remembers flashcards from our childhood days. The fronts of the cards had math equations, words, science terms, or images, and the backs had the "answer"— the solution, definition, explanation, or whatever response the student was expected to give.

The idea of flashcards sprouts from this concept. This approach is neither new nor very complicated: it's simply recalling information you've already learned (the back of the flashcard) when prompted by a certain image or depiction (the front).

Retrieval practice is one of the best ways to increase your memory and fact retention. But even though its core is quite simple, actually using retrieval practice isn't quite as straightforward as just passively using flashcards or scanning over notes we've taken. Rather, retrieval practice is an active skill: truly struggling, thinking, and processing to finally get to the point of recalling that information without clues—much of what we've discussed already in this book that accelerates learning.

Pooja Agarwal researched pupils taking middle school social studies over the course of a year and a half, ending in 2011. The study aimed to determine how regularly scheduled, uncounted quizzes—basically, retrieval practice exercises—benefitted the ability to learn and retain.

The class teacher didn't alter their study plan and simply instructed as normal. The students were given regular quizzes—developed by the research team—on class material with the understanding that the results would *not* count against their grades.

These quizzes only covered about a third of the material covered by the teacher, who also had to leave the room while the quiz was being taken by the students. This was so the teacher had no knowledge of what subjects the quizzes covered. During class, the teacher taught and reviewed the class as usual, without knowing which parts of the instruction were being asked on the quizzes.

The results of this study were measured during end-of-unit exams and were dramatic. Students scored one full grade level higher on the material the quizzes covered—the one-third of what the whole class covered—than the questions *not* covered on the no-stakes quizzes. The mere act of being occasionally tested, with no pressure to get all the answers right to boost their overall grades, actually helped students learn better.

Agarwal's study provided insight on what kind of questions helped the most. Questions that required the student to actually recall the information from scratch yielded more success than multiple-choice questions, in which the answer could be recognized from a list, or true/false questions. The active mental effort to remember the answer, with no verbal or visual prompt, improved the students' learning and retention.

The principal benefit of retrieval practice is that it encourages an *active* exertion of effort rather than the passive seepage of external information.

If we pull concepts *out* of our brain, it's more effective than just continually trying to put concepts *in*. The learning comes from taking what's been added to our knowledge and bringing it out at a later time. We mentioned flashcards earlier and how they're an offshoot of retrieval practice. But flashcards are not, in and of themselves, the strategy: you *can* use them and still not be conducting true retrieval practice.

Many students use flashcards inactively: they see the prompt, answer it in their heads, tell themselves they know it, flip over to see the answer, and then move on to the next one. Turning this into *practice*, however, would be taking a few seconds to actually recall the answer and, at best, to say the answer out loud before flipping the card over. The difference seems slight and subtle, but it's important. Students will get more advantages from flashcards by actually retrieving and vocalizing the answer before moving on. Forcing yourself into situations like using flashcards and practice tests is what makes you remember at your best.

In real-world situations—where there's usually not an outside teacher, premade flashcards, or other assistance—how can we repurpose what we learn for retrieval practice? One good way is to expand flashcards to make them more "interactive."

The flashcards in our grade-school experiences, for the most part, were very one-note. You can adapt the methodology of flashcards for more complex, real-world applications or self-learning by taking a new approach to what's on the back of the cards.

When you're studying material for work or class, make flashcards with concepts on the front and definitions on the back. After completing this task, make another set of cards that give "instructions" on how to reprocess the concept for a creative or real-life situation. Here's an example:

- "Rewrite this concept in only one sentence."

- "Write a movie or novel plot that demonstrates this concept."

- "Use this concept to describe a real-life event."

- "Describe the *opposite* of this concept."

The possibilities are, as they say, limitless in how you can seek retrieval. Remember, your goal is to require yourself to reach into your memory, display the information, and only then put it back.

In order to make the best use of your flashcards, commit to making two sets. The first set will contain mere definitions and single concepts: one-word prompts for one-word or one-sentence answers.

The second set of flashcards will contain as much information about a single concept as possible so you will be forced to recall all of that with the prompt of a single word. This is also known as chunking information, where it's advantageous to your short-term memory (which can only hold on average seven items) to remember information as a large chunk rather than as smaller, individual components. This means that when you put more information on each flashcard, that set of information becomes one item versus five items.

When you go through your flashcards, put the cards you got wrong back into the middle or front of your stack so you see them sooner and more frequently. This helps you work through your mistakes and commit them to memory more quickly.

Using these exercises extracts more information about the concept that you produce yourself. Placing them in context of a creative narrative or expression will help you understand them when they come up in real life. Retrieval practice is simple enough with flashcards and essentially testing yourself. When you make your brain sweat a little to dig the information out of your memory and practice retrieval, you'll find that information sticks in your head extremely well. Get fancy with flashcards and prompt for information that will test the limits of your understanding and knowledge. What's important is to keep drawing the information *out*, and your memory will greatly improve.

Takeaways:

- Information retention is the act of using your brain like a sponge. You can absorb and synthesize something, but if it doesn't stay in your brain, then it's truly a useless pursuit. You aren't able to apply it, use it, or whip it out on tests. What's the point? So it has to stick. Luckily, brain science is particularly useful here in knowing what helps us

retain information, and it's probably not what you've been doing on your own.
- Emotion is a powerful information retention tool. This is because our brains are wired to prefer emotional, vivid, and outlier information. It helped keep us alive, it's more engaging, and it just tends to stick more easily. Thus, if we can associate information with emotion, vivid imagery, memorable stories (of your own creation), then we stand a better chance of retaining. There are simply more subconscious hooks for our conscious brain to pluck information from our memory banks; emotion is a considerable hook.
- Memory is best built actively and with struggle and discomfort. In this way, it's like the physical body and the pain of exercise—if your workouts consist of 15 minutes of walking, then you're likely not building very much. Thus, passive methods of learning like summarization, highlighting, and even mnemonics have not proven to be very effective. Instead, the next two methods were shown to have the most effectiveness.

- Spaced repetition implores you to focus on frequency rather than duration of learning. This has been proven to be more effective than most other conventional study schedules. This is why cramming during an all-nighter doesn't work so well and why planning your study schedule is of utmost importance.
- Finally, utilize self-testing and practicing drawing information out of your brain instead of trying to stuff information into it. This may be counterintuitive, but the more we can engage in mini tests, the better we memorize and learn. This is known as retrieval practice, as you are retrieving information. Though this is mostly done through the context of flashcards, the overarching lesson is that we must be active in our efforts. The bigger the struggle, the deeper the learning and memorization. When you force yourself to learn, well, you will learn. There is no real shortcut.

Summary Guide

Chapter 1. The Learning Brain

- To learn better, we need to tap into the learning brain that already exists inside of us. This involves understanding how our brain prefers to accept information and working with it instead of trying to cram information inside it like a clown car. In truth, there are always two brains waging war inside us: the prefrontal cortex, which allows us to learn, and the limbic system, which robs us of our senses. Of course, this is a problem that affects far more about our behavior than learning, but it is the first stop on our journey to neuro-learning.
- In the end, we have three primary areas of focus that we can derive from brain physiology: information absorption (literally being able to process and intake information), information synthesis (the ability to analyze,

comprehend, and make meaningful), and information retention (memorization and encoding).
- For the last element of retention, we also dive into the three steps of creating a memory, which are encoding, storage, and retrieval. A failure to satisfy any of those steps will lead to quicker forgetting and the overall feeling that you haven't quite learned something.
- Before we dive into techniques that our brain enjoys, we take a quick look at the psychological prerequisites to learning. This is summed up in the learning success pyramid, where we find that confidence (I can do this) and self-management (I will make a plan for how to do this) are paramount to effective learning. We could even go as far as to say that they are prerequisites to learning; how are you going to learn to speak Norwegian if you can't create a coherent plan for learning and also believe that it is within your abilities to do so?

Chapter 2. Information Absorption

- Information absorption is the first key to effective learning that caters to our brains. If we cannot see, hear, or perceive a piece of information, forget about the rest of the process. No number of memory techniques or amount of deep learning will make a difference if the information hasn't made it into your head.

- The first step to ensuring that we can properly absorb information is to look at the cognitive load that we place on our brains. There are three types of loads: intrinsic, extrinsic, and germane. They have to do with how difficult the information is, how the information is present, and how difficult the information is to turn into something with personal significance. The brain is mighty, but still biological and in need of plenty of rest, breaks, and light cognitive loads. Another way to look at it is that we can only choose two of the following three elements: *intensity*, *frequency*, and *duration.*

- Chunking is a magnificent way to lighten the cognitive load and assist in information absorption because it literally turns 10 pieces of information into three (for example). The simple ways for chunking to help all three elements of the learning process are to chunk based on groupings, categories, and patterns—all of which you can arbitrarily create. Effective ways to chunk information for better absorption and synthesis (and also retention) are to map new information onto old information and tear it down to the smallest subparts possible, which means that you are breaking something down so you can chunk it together in a way that is significant to you.

- Something that makes the brain unable to pay attention, focus, or care about anything at all is stress. We covered this briefly in the first chapter when we looked at the brain's components and the limbic system in particular. When the brain is under stress, everything shuts down. And yet, we cannot function without a small level of stress; this assertion is governed by the Yerkes-Dodson upside-down U curve, which dictates that we all have a so-called sweet spot in terms of stress for best mental performance. Not too much, but not so little so as to stay engaged.

- Finally, when it comes to information absorption, we must be resourceful in finding ways to capture attention and engagement. This is where mixing and matching different learning styles and mediums comes into play. It's not necessarily that any of these styles and mediums are scientifically better than others, but sometimes we can burn out, grow bored, or simply not care when something is presented in a way that we don't like or prefer. Thus, we present a couple of different models for different styles and mediums: active versus reflective, sensing versus intuitive, visual versus verbal/other, and sequential versus global, as well as the dubious knowledge of the learning pyramid, which contains listening, reading, audio/visual, demonstration, discussion, real-life experience, and teaching others. Remember, the myth of learning styles is just that—a myth.

Chapter 3. Information Synthesis

- Information synthesis is the second branch of effective learning in a way that our brain likes. Synthesis, or comprehension and understanding by other names, is probably the true bedrock of what we would usually consider learning. It's taking on a new concept or set of information and knowing it inside and out. It's knowing the context it fits in and seeing it from as many angles as possible to ensure that understanding is true and thorough, especially with regard to blind spots. That sounds like a tall order, and it is. But it's this very struggle and slog that cements understanding and retention. It's not necessarily "no pain, no gain" but the brain simply sees no reason to remember something if there is no apparent reason to (i.e., it is not forced to work for it).
- Bloom's taxonomy is a wonderful tool for understanding and manipulating

information. It's a sequence of thought elements that go into deep synthesis. In fact, each of the six phases imparts a guideline for how to interact with information more deeply to ensure comprehension. Before you can understand a concept, you must remember it. To apply a concept, you must first understand it. In order to evaluate a process, you must have analyzed it. To create an accurate conclusion, you must have completed a thorough evaluation. The challenge is introspection and understanding where you currently fall on the taxonomy, because only then can you understand what is required for you to move forward in your understanding.

- The SQ3R method is another tool for better understanding. It's about interacting with the resources you use for learning. Where most people may read or listen to something once and call it a day, the SQ3R stands for survey, question, read, recite, and review. That's roughly five layers of analysis for you to grow your understanding. We learn

better when we know what's ahead and when we know what just occurred.
- Self-explanation (elaborative interrogation) and the Feynman technique are the final tools for better information synthesis. When we are forced to try to explain concepts through self-inquiry, we will quickly discover what we do know and what we don't know at all. These are called blind spots, and they are far more common than you might like to think. Can you explain why the sky is blue or how gravity works? Probably not off the top of your head, even though you think you understand those concepts. The Feynman technique is an offshoot of self-explanation that helps find blind spots as well, with an added component of using an analogy to explain what you think you know. This is probably the most powerful tool because it instantly makes you feel ignorant—a positive thing in the realm of learning.

Chapter 4. Information Retention

- Information retention is the act of using your brain like a sponge. You can absorb and synthesize something, but if it doesn't stay in your brain, then it's truly a useless pursuit. You aren't able to apply it, use it, or whip it out on tests. What's the point? So it has to stick. Luckily, brain science is particularly useful here in knowing what helps us retain information, and it's probably not what you've been doing on your own.
- Emotion is a powerful information retention tool. This is because our brains are wired to prefer emotional, vivid, and outlier information. It helped keep us alive, it's more engaging, and it just tends to stick more easily. Thus, if we can associate information with emotion, vivid imagery, memorable stories (of your own creation), then we stand a better chance of retaining. There are simply more subconscious hooks for our conscious brain to pluck information from our memory banks; emotion is a considerable hook.

- Memory is best built actively and with struggle and discomfort. In this way, it's like the physical body and the pain of exercise—if your workouts consist of 15 minutes of walking, then you're likely not building very much. Thus, passive methods of learning like summarization, highlighting, and even mnemonics have not proven to be very effective. Instead, the next two methods were shown to have the most effectiveness.
- Spaced repetition implores you to focus on frequency rather than duration of learning. This has been proven to be more effective than most other conventional study schedules. This is why cramming during an all-nighter doesn't work so well and why planning your study schedule is of utmost importance.
- Finally, utilize self-testing and practicing drawing information out of your brain instead of trying to stuff information into it. This may be counterintuitive, but the more we can engage in mini tests, the better we memorize and learn. This is known as retrieval practice, as you are

retrieving information. Though this is mostly done through the context of flashcards, the overarching lesson is that we must be active in our efforts. The bigger the struggle, the deeper the learning and memorization. When you force yourself to learn, well, you will learn. There is no real shortcut.

www.ingramcontent.com/pod-product-compliance
Lightning Source LLC
Chambersburg PA
CBHW071200070526
44584CB00019B/2861